Walking in the Countryside

Walking in the Countryside

David Sharp

in collaboration with the
Ramblers Association

David & Charles
Newton Abbot   London   North Pomfret(VT)
Vancouver

British Library Cataloguing in Publication Data

Sharp, David
    Walking in the Countryside.
        1. Walking—Great Britain
        I. Title II. Ramblers' Association
    796.5'1'0941   GV199.44.G7

    ISBN 0-7153-7495-8

Library of Congress Catalog Card Number 77-85013

First published 1978
Second impression 1978

© David Sharp 1978

Printed in Great Britain
by Biddles of Guildford
for David & Charles (Publishers) Limited
Brunel House   Newton Abbot   Devon

Published in the United States of America
by David & Charles Inc
North Pomfret   Vermont 05053   USA

Published in Canada
by Douglas David & Charles Limited
1875 Welch Street   North Vancouver   BC

Contents

Preface

Taking a walk in the country has become probably the most popular of all simple leisure-time activities. Millions have tried it, perhaps by sampling their local footpaths or by setting out to follow the instructions in a guide they have chanced on in a local bookshop. Many have the feeling that they are only just touching on the many pleasures of country walking; that there must be so much more to explore if they only knew how. This book aims to help by answering the following questions. How did the paths get there? What is their status? How do you find them? Where are the best walking areas? In compiling all the information I have had the able help of John Newnham and John Trevelyan, assistant secretaries of the Ramblers' Association. The footpath rights of way are a significant and unique part of our island heritage, so it is appropriate that our first two chapters, contributed by Alan Mattingly, the Association's national secretary, should paint a broad picture of their past and recent history. We hope that through our book you will find a richer experience in exploring the countryside.

1 The Unique Heritage

Standing on Whitehorse Hill on the Great Ridgeway, at a point 18 miles south-west of Oxford and over 850ft above sea level, it is easy to appreciate the imprints of history on the English landscape. On the steep north-facing scarp of the chalk downs, 150ft below, is the White Horse itself—a beautiful but enigmatic creation some 360ft in length, which may be as old as the Neolithic or as recent as King Alfred; and to your left is the large but relatively shallow hill fort of Uffington Castle, generally thought to be of Iron Age origin, but possibly of a much earlier date. But the feature in this landscape that is probably far older than any other is the Ridgeway itself. This wide rutted track strides confidently along the main ridge of the downs and extends as far as the eye can see to east and west. It would have been an ancient monument in the time of the Romans, having been in use since the sub-Arctic climate of the last Ice Age began to ameliorate over 10,000 years ago.

If the weather is typically clear and windy, you will see, beyond the Ridgeway to the north and south, landscapes of great contrast. To the south are the downs, with their wide expansive ridges and their deep streamless valleys. Along many of the ridges you will be able to pick out the courses of other tracks similar to, if rather less distinguished-looking than, the Ridgeway itself. Today many of these tracks are green lanes or bridleways, used partly as means of access to the large farm buildings standing alone on the downs, but also, like the Ridgeway, as important recreation routes for the country-lovers of the twentieth century. These tracks, if followed more carefully on the map, are seen to connect not only the farm buildings and the settlements in the valleys, but also with the tumuli, the hill forts and the Roman villas, which are scattered in seemingly random fashion about the hills and valleys. This connection between the tracks and the ancient features testifies to the antiquity of so many rights of way in Britain—a unique heritage indeed.

The Ridgeway climbs the Berkshire Downs to the earth ramparts
of Uffington Castle on the skyline

The same quality of timelessness is apparent in the scenery and
the paths to the north of our viewpoint on Whitehorse Hill.
Looking across the flat fertile Vale of White Horse, we can pick
out the clustered villages, with their small but delightful
churches; the hamlets and the farmsteads surrounded by their
lush green pastures and fields of billowing corn; and the narrow
country lanes weaving their way from one settlement to the
next.

In addition, with the aid of a pair of binoculars and a good
map, you may be able to pick out the routes of some other rights
of way which, although often no less ancient than the tracks on
the downs to the south, are entirely different in nature. These
are the paths that the villagers and farmers of medieval times
used on their way to work in the fields, on their way to church,
or just to visit friends and neighbours. Some of these paths may
have been lost when the open fields were enclosed in later

centuries; others may have come into being as trade between the different regions of Britain increased, and there were large-scale movements of cattle, sheep and goods along the drove roads and tracks that today stand silent and overgrown.

The mists of time obscure the origin of most of today's paths and tracks. Nevertheless it is clear that a great many of them, like the Ridgeway, are very old indeed. As the ice sheets retreated, and as the Stone Age hunting tribes of Europe moved northwards across Britain, they would have followed the paths —or at least the terrain—of least resistance. The clay vales of the Thames Basin and the Weald carried dense oak forest until well into the Middle Ages, but the chalk downlands carried, at most, only a light and easily penetrated beech woodland. The long unbroken chalk ridges also favoured fast migration, and it is not surprising that it is on the North and South Downs, and on the chalk hills of Berkshire, Dorset, Lincolnshire and York-shire, that some of the oldest and most clearly defined rights of way are to be found.

The ridges offered the safest and the quickest routes, but the lack of water was (and to today's long-distance walker still is) a problem, so that other routes were established lower down the scarp face on the spring line. Thus the ancient Icknield Way, which can be traced in one form or another from the Thames near Goring right along the foot of the chalk scarp into Norfolk, came into being as an important prehistoric route. The Pilgrims' Way to Canterbury along the foot of the North Downs scarp offers another example, although some would dispute that such a track was ever used by medieval pilgrims travelling to the shrine of Thomas à Becket.

Some of our tracks and paths give evidence of Roman origin, because these were often constructed with special materials and to a distinctive design, and were, as everyone knows, laid down in straight lines as far as possible. The Romans built over 5,000 miles of military road in Britain, and although many of their routes are today followed by motor roads—Watling Street and parts of the Fosse Way for example—many are not, and offer traffic-free routes for the walker and horserider. Indeed, one of the best-preserved stretches of Roman road is to be found high

11

on Wheeldale Moor, west of Whitby, far away from the modern A-road that crosses the North York Moors. Again, one of the most exhilarating ridge walks in the Lake District follows the Roman road—appropriately named High Street—from Trout-beck to Penrith, rising to no less than 2,700ft above sea level.

In lower country the remaining unmetalled roads of Roman origin often provide walking routes of great charm and variety. Ten miles south-east of Cambridge, near a village called Horseheath, you can pick up a track which, after a little early meandering, heads straight back to that city, passing smoothly over the undulating downs until it breaks out on to the Gog Magog hills, where you can enjoy what is probably the finest view of Cambridge and its university. The Romans themselves would only have seen a few windswept buildings and some fortifications of no great distinction, but they certainly chose their point of entry with some attention to the lie of the land.

Of a less dramatic character is the unmetalled stretch of Ermine Street between Cheshunt and Hertford on the northern border

Walkers follow the Roman road on High Street in the Lake District

of London. What was for the Romans the beginning of a vital link between Londinium and Lindum Colonia (Lincoln) is today an intensively used recreational route running the breadth of the city's Green Belt.

The Romans' main routes are well known, but they must also have constructed (or simply trod out) a great many local routes that yet remain to be traced by historians and archaeologists. Where the necessary intensive research has been done, as by I. D. Margary in his *Roman Ways in the Weald*, it has been shown that a great many of our existing paths and tracks are of Roman origin.

The network of communications the Romans built up was important for another reason. Professor Hoskins points out in his *The Making of the English Landscape* that 'they opened up in their time whole tracts of the countryside on a scale hitherto unknown. Even the lesser local roads pushed through the forested clay lands in all directions, and crossed the high moorlands'. Although many of these Roman ways became neglected after the Romans left Britain and the Dark Ages settled in, many of them must have provided important routes for the Saxons, Danes and Normans. These invaders would have used the Roman routes not only as military roads but also as points of entry into the forests, which they set about clearing with axe and fire.

The fifth to the eleventh centuries saw the creation of the greater part of today's pattern of rural settlement; and as the forests were cleared and the villages and hamlets established, so too were lines of communication laid down. People had two principal means of travel—on foot or on horseback. Few villagers travelled far beyond their settlement, and the main patterns of movement were highly local in nature.

With the open-field system, which was such a major feature of manorial England, people tramped out paths to take them from their cottages to their field strips, and from one village to another. The church being a powerful influence in the land, it soon came about that some of the most heavily used tracks were those leading to the place of worship.

It is important to remember that this semi-primitive agricultural way of life, with its associated patterns of settlement and

13

communication, lasted in many areas for several centuries. In fact the record of the *Domesday Book* shows us that our present rural settlement pattern had become largely (though by no means entirely) established by the time William the Conquerer landed at Hastings. It was a way of life that was to continue unchanged in many parts of Britain until as late as the eighteenth century. Imagine then how people must have regarded the rights of way established by the early settlers and used by generation after generation without let or hindrance. People of all classes must have regarded them as indisputable rights of passage that no one would dare question. As time went by, as field patterns changed, and as villages grew or shrank or even disappeared altogether, the paths that had been in use for centuries remained as routes which everyone was entitled to follow. So it has remained until the present day—up to a point.

Boundaries of kingdoms and parishes alike are also often followed by well delineated paths. Hoskins describes a 'hollow way' in Cheriton Bishop, Devon, where a track drops down a steep hillside between ancient earth banks several feet high, and he attributes this feature to the fact that the way was dug out in some pre-Saxon age to mark the boundary between two Celtic landowners. Several parish boundaries are followed in places by similar 'hollow ways' and other paths. Although their value as communication links may have been limited, they were often followed by the parishioners once each year in ceremonies known as 'beating the bounds', a custom some enthusiastic rambling groups are trying to revive at the present day.

More extensive were the boundaries between warring factions. Offa's Dyke (on the Welsh border) and the Wansdyke (on the Wiltshire Downs) were defensive features in their time, but today (and probably for the many centuries since their defensive role became obsolete) they are followed by rights of way. Even Hadrian's Wall is today followed by the Pennine Way and other paths for much of its length.

The significance of drove roads and other medieval trade routes should also not be underestimated. Once England and Wales had become a united kingdom, free from serious internal civil war, large-scale movements of animals and goods, particularly towards

Ancient ways meet at Kidhow Gate, Yorkshire. The sign marks the point where the Pennine Way leaves the Cam High Road, a Roman road, to follow the old packhorse track northwards to Hawes. Ingleborough towers in the distance

London, began to be established. For example, cattle were moved from the Welsh hills into the English lowlands for fattening and thence to the main market towns. The drove roads used for this purpose often followed established tracks and lanes of local origin, but in some cases new links were needed. In any event, the routes soon acquired a character of their own. Where they have not been subsequently metalled over, these trackways today exist as some of the most delightful of our green lanes. Brian Smith in his book *The Cotswolds* describes a track called the Welsh Way 3 miles north-east of Cirencester, which is 'a delightful lane meandering between hedges filled with dog rose and through tunnels of woodland'. He explains that the Way got its name because it was used 'by the Welsh drovers bringing their black cattle out of Wales by way of Gloucester and the Cotswolds to the Thames Valley where they were fattened before being taken on to Smithfield for the Christmas market'.

Running roughly parallel with the Welsh Way across the

15

Cotswolds are a number of other tracks and lanes of similar origin. On today's OS map their names are recorded—'Calf Way', 'Salt Way', and so forth. The salt ways of England have attracted particular attention, because salt would have been an important commodity in the development of long-distance routes. It was cheap to produce, easy to transport, localised in supply and widespread in demand. Cheshire has for long been an important source of salt, and salt ways have been found to radiate away from places like Droitwich, particularly south-eastwards across the West Midlands.

In England the enclosure movement was well under way by the beginning of the eighteenth century, although the process of replacing the open-strip fields with single enclosures was often by no means the dramatic process it is often pictured as being, and many of the old rights of way associated with the pre-enclosure field pattern remain to this day. But where enclosure was delayed until the eighteenth or nineteenth centuries—as in much of the East Midlands, for instance—the change was usually abrupt. Enclosure commissioners went round the country redrawing the field pattern and trying to apportion the fields fairly between those who were to remain. Some of the old paths were retained, but many became overgrown through lack of use, and were eventually lost altogether. Many new roads and tracks were created, and these are often found to be wide and straight in nature, difficult to distinguish perhaps from the routes of Roman origin unless you are able to check them on the enclosure award map.

The enclosure movement was part of an Agricultural Revolution that was being carried out more or less simultaneously with the Industrial Revolution. That Revolution, with its massive shift of population from the country into the burgeoning towns and cities, was to create within a relatively short space of time an entirely new role and an entirely new set of conflicts for the paths and lanes that threaded through the countryside.

The age of mass recreation was beginning to dawn.

2 The Paths Today

On a dull grey November day in 1976 a group of 250 people assembled at the end of an undistinguished cinder footpath running between a railway line and a golf course in the equally undistinguished suburb of Flixton in Manchester. They were there to celebrate the setting up, 150 years ago, of one of the earliest recorded footpath protection societies in Britain. It was on 15 November 1826 that a public meeting was held in the Town Hall, Manchester, at which the Manchester Association for the Preservation of Ancient Footpaths was established. Its immediate purpose was to save a footpath known as 'The Bottoms', which Squire Ralph Wright of Flixton House wanted to dispose of.

The Manchester Association was successful in this battle (hence the celebrations in Flixton 150 years later), and went on to other victories; but the conflict that brought it into existence epitomised the new situation the Industrial Revolution was creating for country paths. Life in Victorian Manchester, as in the many other expanding industrial towns and cities, was grim; the number of townsfolk was growing rapidly, as more moved into the cities from the rural areas where they could no longer find work. The factory workers and their families had precious little free time, and even less spare cash with which to enjoy their 'leisure hours', but during that time they often used to get out of their urban surroundings altogether by the simple expedient of going for a walk in the countryside.

By the middle of the century there were more people living in the towns than in the country, and the demand for open-air recreation was growing rapidly. The ancient tracks of the Neolithic pastoralists, the Roman legions and the Saxon forest-clearers became the Victorian worker's escape route from the oppressiveness of his daily toil. However, those who were left in the rural communities (or at least the wealthier ones among them) viewed this weekend invasion of their fields and footpaths

17

with some alarm. Their privacy was invaded, or so they thought, and their crops were at risk. Attempts were made to close down footpaths, and it was possible in the early part of the nineteenth century for this to be done with the agreement of two magistrates, without any need for a public hearing.

The reaction from the townsfolk was strong and swift. At first it came predominantly from the up-and-coming middle classes, who were, for example, primarily responsible for the setting up of the Manchester Association in 1826. But the feeling against this tampering with ancient rights ran deep, and before the country squires had time to organise themselves properly, Parliament had passed the Highways Act of 1835, which gave wide protection to rights of way of all kinds and lay at the heart of all footpath legislation right up until 1949.

In the second half of the nineteenth century the popularity of walking in the countryside continued to grow, and with this growth came the setting up of a host of local rambling clubs, footpath societies and other outdoor organisations. Some still exist today, like the London-based Forest Ramblers, established in 1884 and still organising the traditional monthly Thursday rambles for elderly and distinguished gentlemen. But the conflicts between town and country did not subside—indeed, they became more accentuated—and the local clubs and societies recognised that there was also a need for national organisations to protect their rights. The first national amenity society to concern itself with outdoor recreation was the Commons, Open Spaces and Footpaths Protection Society, set up in 1865. It fought a long, hard and expensive battle to keep Epping Forest open and unenclosed. That battle was also successful, and the Society continues its work to the present day. In fact the value of open spaces and common land in and around the cities was officially recognised from this time on by the passing of such legislation as the Commons Acts of 1876 and 1899, the Open Spaces Act of 1906, and section 193 of the Law of Property Act 1925 which gave the public a right to roam at will over all common land lying within borough and urban districts. This allowed access to many of our familiar town commons, but in one or two areas it also afforded public access to some extensive and important rural areas that happened to fall within an urban district: for example, much of central Lake District is today open for public access because it formerly came within the boundary of Windermere UD or Lakes UD.

By the turn of the century the local clubs and societies were beginning to organise themselves into federations better to defend their interests. In 1905 the first of these, the Southern Federation of Rambling Clubs, was set up in London. Later, during the 1920s, other federations were set up in centres such as Manchester and Sheffield.

The clubs and the federations continued to draw their support almost solely from the industrial towns and cities. People were still eager to get away from the smoke and the slums whenever they could, and their discovery of rural peace and beauty became an inspiration for greater and greater numbers. Tom Stephenson, who was later to become Secretary of the Ramblers' Association, described his first experience of the open air as a lad of 13 in 1904, standing on the summit of Pendle Hill, 2,000ft above the textile factories and industrial towns of north-east Lancashire, in which he had hitherto spent nearly all his waking hours:

It was breathtaking. I saw range after range of snow-capped hills—Ingleborough, Penyghent, all of which I didn't know then, but which were to become old friends.

I just hadn't realised that this whole new world was on my doorstep. I made up my mind that day that this was for me.

His feelings were shared by many others. It was their enthusiasm and their conviction that all members of the community were entitled, as of right, to enjoy the delights of walking in the countryside that provided the driving force for the organisation of the open-air movement at this time.

The value of country paths as a recreational asset had become firmly established, and the clubs and federations were busy promoting their enjoyment by arranging walks, scouting around for suitable transport and accommodation. Where they could not find it, they took steps to provide it themselves by building youth hostels and organising rail and coach excursions. Conflicts over footpaths in this period were not unduly bitter or great in number. Sporadic attempts were still being made to close paths here and there, and the lack of signposting and waymarking was a handicap. But the agricultural industry was not in a buoyant state, and footpaths and ramblers were not seen, as they are sometimes portrayed today, as threats to the nation's food supply. It was not until after World War II, when agriculture became much more intensive and productive, that footpaths became a matter of major national dispute.

What did hit the headlines in the Thirties were the militant campaigns for access to the jealously guarded grouse moors of Derbyshire, Yorkshire and Lancashire. The celebrated case in which a number of ramblers were imprisoned for a time after a confrontation with gamekeepers on a mass trespass on Kinder Scout was but one incident—though perhaps the most dramatic —in a turbulent series of attempts to reassert what the trespassers regarded as a basic human right.

The trespass campaign paid off in the end, but not in the way the campaigners hoped or foresaw, because the legislation on which all hopes were pinned—the Access to Mountains Bill of 1939— was totally emasculated by the Bill's opponents, and it had no positive benefit at all. Again, it was not until 1949 that effective powers to provide public access to open country were created by Parliament. However, the access campaign attracted a lot of support and one of its indirect results was to foster the setting up of a national body to protect the interest of walkers. In 1931 the various rambling federations agreed to set up a national organisation, and in 1935 this emerged with the title, the Ramblers' Association.

The Post-war Period

It is perhaps a curious irony that the one historical event which more than anything else was responsible for the creation of national parks, and the very wide-ranging changes in footpath legislation we have seen in recent years, was World War II. After the war there was a great spirit of national reconstruction, and one important aspect of this was the movement to designate certain areas of outstanding scenic attraction and to make them and the rest of the countryside accessible to everyone. The campaigns for access, national parks and footpath protection that had been carried on in the inter-war period were given a new lease of life, and gained tremendous popular support.

The government of the day recognised this and made early plans for national legislation. In 1943 a Ministry of Town and County Planning was created. Shortly afterwards, the new Ministry commissioned John Dower to prepare a report on National Parks in England and Wales, and this was published in 1945. Dower's report, which attracted instant acclaim, has been regarded ever since as one of the most important official documents on access and national parks ever to have been produced. It was very fitting that, nearly 30 years later, the Countryside Commission should name its fine new headquarters in Cheltenham John Dower House.

Dower concentrated his attention on a definition for national parks, and on the areas that might be designated as such. But he also had something to say about footpaths and access. He argued that there was a need for a thorough recasting of footpath law and administration, followed by a systematic nationwide campaign to provide, record, equip and maintain an ample extent of public paths in all districts. On access to the conflict-ridden grouse moors, he said: 'When the issue is seen as a broad question of principle—whether the recreational needs of the many should or should not outweigh the sporting pleasures of the few—there can be little doubt of the answer: that walkers should, sooner or later, be given freedom of access over grouse moors.'

If the post-war outdoor movement gained its popular support from the spirit of national revival, and if it acquired intellectual respect through the Dower Report, then the instrument that brought its campaigns to the point of implementation was the Hobhouse Committee. Set up in 1945, the Hobhouse Committee produced recommendations for giving legislative effect to Dower's philosophy and proposals. In particular the Footpaths and Access Sub-committee produced a series of recommendations giving official endorsement to many of the demands which the Ramblers'

21

Association and others had been making since the Twenties and Thirties.

Their recommendations were based on a sober analysis of the problems relating to access to the countryside. The countryside, they said, should be a national playground for air and exercise for the 40 million townsfolk of this country. In many areas access was debarred. There were too many areas where visitors ran the risk of being turned off open moorland by owners or their agents, by water-gathering authorities or by service departments. 'Uncounted country footpaths have been ploughed up and lost perhaps for all time', they said. Referring to battles fought in the previous century, they argued: 'As the urban dweller fought in the past for his urban commons and open spaces, so he and the countryman need today to agree together how best to achieve fuller public use of the countryside through footpaths and access to uncultivated land.'

With such brave statements as these, the Sub-committee proceeded to enunciate its proposals. It was of fundamental import-

In the 1950s ramblers helped to prepare the first definitive maps, surveying footpaths in Coquetdale. Note the Cheviots in the distance

ance to have a complete survey of all footpaths, bridleways and green lanes. This recommendation led directly to the sections in the 1949 National Parks and Access to the Countryside Act requiring local authorities to produce definitive maps of rights of way so that everyone would know what were and what were not public paths.

Highway authorities, said the Sub-committee, should be required by statute to repair and maintain all rights of way. They should also have duties to prosecute anyone obstructing a public path, to signpost footpaths, and to require the removal of misleading notices. The grazing of bulls in fields containing public paths should be prohibited.

The Sub-committee also commended the concept of long-distance routes and said that the proposed National Parks Commission should be responsible for their creation. It endorsed the list of suggested long-distance routes put forward by the Ramblers' Association some years previously. These included the Pennine Way; a route along the Chiltern escarpment and the Berkshire Ridgeway down to the Devon coast; a path along the line of the 'Pilgrims' Way' from Winchester to Canterbury; another to follow Offa's Dyke on the Welsh border; and further long-distance paths along all sections of undeveloped coastline following the old coastguard tracks.

Many of these proposals were included in the 1949 Act, which had many shortcomings but was undoubtedly the most important piece of legislation to reach the statute book from the country-goer's point of view. Even so, it is sobering to recall that at one stage the government seriously contemplated the possibility of not introducing it at all and giving priority to other Bills. It was only by intensive lobbying of MPs and ministers that the outdoor movement ensured the introduction and passage of the Bill. Perhaps one of the most imaginative exercises in this campaign was the Pennine Way walk that Tom Stephenson arranged for MPs Hugh Dalton, Barbara Castle, Arthur Blenkinsop, George Chetwynd, Geoffrey de Freitas and Fred Willey in 1948. At the end of the trek, from Middleton-in-Teesdale to the Roman Wall, Hugh Dalton (later to become Chancellor of the Exchequer) had enough breath left to say:

Fig 1 The long distance paths and National Parks of England and
Wales, plus other landscape areas reviewed in chapters 8 and 9

24

After renewing acquaintance with this beautiful part of the country, I am sure that we must in the lifetime of this Parliament place on the Statute Book a great measure of liberation, freeing for the health and enjoyment of all our people what for so long has been monopolised for a few. National Parks, so long talked about, must be brought into being. The law regarding rights of way must be clarified and strengthened to remove the bias in favour of the land-lord and to prevent the public losing, through sharp practice or neglect, rights of way to which they are entitled. Subject always to full recognition of the needs of agriculture and forestry, the public should have free and unquestioned access to mountain and moorland and all the wilder parts of Britain.

We stand also for completion of the Pennine Way, remembering that this splendid project was first outlined by our good friend Tom Stephenson in 1935. That was thirteen years ago. We have waited long enough.

Dalton would no doubt have been horrified if he had known then that it would be another 17 years before the Pennine Way was to be officially opened at Malham.

The 1949 Act itself did make it however, despite difficulties, and of course it heralded a new era. But it soon became apparent that the thinking behind the Act had underestimated the signifi-cance of a number of social and economic trends that were to have a great influence on countryside recreation in subsequent years. One of these developments was the phenomenal growth in car ownership. Another was the increase in the amount of leisure time people had at their disposal. Taken together, these two factors led to an explosion of demand for outdoor recreation the size and nature of which had not been foreseen by Dower, Hobhouse or any other official group concerned with the drafting of post-war legislation.

More cars led to a demand for more roads and motorways, and these in turn made more countryside more accessible to more people. This cycle of greater accessibility led to very considerable pressures on popular countryside, and recreation managers in national parks and elsewhere found themselves with the need to provide such facilities as car parks, toilets, nature trails, guided walks and so on, and to combat the problems of litter, erosion, noise and traffic congestion these ever-growing numbers of visitors created.

Increased motor traffic also led to a revival of support for public paths from a section of the population that had so far played no part in the outdoor campaigns. Rural communities started to take an interest. Country lanes became too dangerous to walk or ride along, and footpaths and bridleways became the villagers' routes for walking with their dogs and their children, and for visiting local churches and neighbours—a revival in fact of the paths' medieval usage. Village footpath societies sprang up and parish councils started to take an interest in signposting and waymarking.

The post-war development of the Ramblers' Association illustrates these developments. From a membership in 1950 of 8,778, almost wholly based in the large towns and cities, and with very few car-owners in its midst, the Association has grown to today's membership of over 30,000, with a fairly wide and even distribution of members throughout England and parts of Scotland and Wales. It has a higher proportion of car-owners among its members than does the population at large, and it has seen the growth since 1950 of 140 local groups, the vast majority of which are outside the conurbations, being based at such places as Bridgwater, Stowmarket and Kendal.

During the same period agriculture underwent very substantial changes, and these too had a profound impact on landscape and access. Its incredible increase in productivity in post-war years has, of course, been achieved through the introduction of intensive and technological methods at a rate that has not been witnessed since the Agricultural Revolution. Hedges have been torn up; many more fields ploughed (and the footpaths with them); barbed wire and electric fencing have been strung systematically across miles of farmland; and the old green lanes have been left to grow over as farm machinery is driven along the newly metalled minor country roads.

These changes led to many problems with rights of way—of

obstructions, ploughed-out paths, and overgrown tracks. They also led to a demand from agricultural circles for a complete 'rationalisation' of the path network, 'to bring it up to date with modern day needs'. On the face of it this argument seemed quite sensible, and indeed it was even adopted by the government in the early Sixties.

However, path users were not so keen on the idea. They were conscious of the long history of many of our footpaths and bridleways, and they were anxious to retain their charm and waywardness. They did not relish the idea of a 'planned network' of paths adapted to new field patterns and landscapes which, they thought, would deprive walking in the countryside of much of its interest. They knew too that the path network had remained intact throughout many changes of history and that today's 'planned network' might become, with agricultural change, tomorrow's 'out of date system'. They preferred the gradual evolution of the path network that had hitherto characterised its development.

They had other suspicions about rationalisation. Such schemes as had been put up tended to reduce the number and mileage of footpaths in an area, and this, of course, the walkers would not tolerate. Creation of missing links and diversions to suit everyone's interest were one thing; the wholesale loss of ancient rights of passage for the benefit of modern agriculture was another.

The debate raged for year after year, but eventually the government climbed down a little, and in its latest policy statement it talks of 'scope for local initiatives to modify the existing networks of footpaths and bridleways in order to reconcile the increasing demands for access for recreation with the needs of the farming community'. Such modification should only be carried out 'on the basis of co-operation between all concerned' and where the object is 'neither to pare down the existing network nor to enlarge it' but to 'adapt' it to everyone's benefit. Historians may agree that such an evolutionary approach towards footpath change is in effect little more than an official endorsement of what has been going on for centuries already.

Such contentious subjects apart, general agreement was reached that further action, particularly in the form of legislation, was needed to take account of these post-1949 developments. Recognising the ever-growing demand for access to open country, the Royal Commission on Common Land recommended in 1958 that, like footpaths, all common land should be registered. They also urged that a right of public access should be extended to all common land. As yet this recommendation has not been implemented, but neither unfortunately has the process of common land registration been completed.

However, the need for more access to open country was not a point that was occupying most people's minds. The main area of concern was how to cope with the rising flood of motorised visitors, not just to the national parks, but also to the countryside generally. Two changes in particular emerged from the think-tanks of the Sixties and were incorporated in the Countryside Act of 1968. One was to enlarge the old National Parks Commission, and transform it into a Countryside Commission, whose remit would cover all non-urban areas and all forms of informal outdoor recreation. The new Commission also commanded significantly greater resources than the old one, and it embarked on a programme of research to provide it with a basis for future policy and action.

On footpaths, one of the most important and interesting of the Commission's pieces of research—the Pennine Way study of 1971—demonstrated that the majority of users of the Way were merely out for a short stroll on a path they could have confidence in. They knew it was there, and that it was likely to be clearly waymarked. This research brought to the Commission's attention the growing demand for clearly identifiable country walks. They have since developed a policy—yet to be effectively implemented because it is so new—which concentrates not so much on the long-distance routes but more on short local paths of most use to the day visitor out with his family for a drive and a short stroll.

A second concept to emerge from the need to cater for the carborne outdoor-seeking masses was the country park—a place where large numbers of people could be absorbed without damage to farming or the landscape, and where the facilities they sought could be provided. By 1976 over 120 country parks had been opened in England and Wales, and there can be no doubt that they provide an outdoor experience for many people who otherwise might never appreciate the beauty of the countryside or the value of the rights of way that pass through it.

The need to review footpath legislation was also recognised in the Sixties, and a special committee under the chairmanship of Sir Arthur Gosling was set up in 1968 to do just this. It made a number of recommendations, but only a few were given effect in the Countryside Act. Many proposals remain officially unconsidered to this day—hardly a very satisfactory state of affairs, bearing in mind that some of the conflicts remain as sharp as ever. However, of those proposals that did get onto the statute book, the most important were those relating to signposting and waymarking. Highway authorities were given a duty to signpost paths where they left metalled roads, and they were also given powers to waymark rights of way along their routes.

Today there are many problems left to solve, but things are improving all the time. Walking in the countryside continues to grow in popularity. Indeed it is generally reckoned that walking ranks alongside angling and football as one of the nation's three most popular recreations. There are more paths in good order today than there have been for many decades; there are more people using them than at any time in the past century; and the opportunities for exploring the countryside are enormous.

The principal resource for this enjoyment of the countryside is the path network, an irreplaceable asset whose origins are as firmly rooted in history as man's civilisation and settlement in this country. This asset should be jealously guarded for future generations and extensively enjoyed by the present one.

3 Rights and Wrongs of Country Paths

The walker on country paths hardly expects to get involved in complex points of highway law. Probably nothing is further from his mind. However, it does help in many ways to have a clear concept of what a public path is, what our rights are, what the law entitles us to do—and what it does not.

We can best start with that term 'right of way'. It is applied to virtually all the paths we follow in the country. Basically it means that you are entitled by right to make your way along a public path—you are not there by permission of the landowner. In this way public footpaths and bridleways are just as much highways in law as major trunk roads, and as such are afforded the same protection by the law. The path may not always be visible on the ground, but you retain your right to walk along it. Even if it has not been used for years, it will keep its status as a right of way—a status that once established can only be taken away by legal process.

It is also important to note, however, that a right of way can exist only along a certain specified route; it is in no way a general right to get from one point to another by any way convenient. That is why it is so important to know the exact line of a path and stick to it. The point is well illustrated by a rather surprising example. If a clifftop or river-bank path is carried away by natural erosion, we have no *right* to solve the problem by taking a route further inland. This is sometimes permitted by a consenting landowner, but in theory the right of way along its single defined route is lost. Further, our right is one of passage only, as genuine travellers. If, as travellers, we feel like stopping for a rest, the law would reasonably allow this, but a full-scale family picnic, for example, would be exceeding our simple right of passage.

Is It a Right of Way?

Now to a critical question. You *think* you are on a public path, but how can you be certain it is a right of way? It is very much easier to answer this question today than it used to be, thanks to a very important piece of legislation, the National Parks and Access to the Countryside Act, which became law in 1949. Up to the time when the provisions of this Act began to have effect, proving the status of a public footpath was all too often a very complicated process.

The law insisted that, for a path to become a right of way, some landowner in the past must have intended to dedicate it as such, and the dedication must have been recognised by the public. So when the status was challenged, perhaps by a landowner intent on closing the path, it was necessary to find evidence that it had in fact been used for so long as to warrant the assumption that a former owner had dedicated a right of way. Parish records and enclosure awards had to be searched, and elderly witnesses persuaded to come forward and testify that for 20 years back, and as far as their memories could reach, local folk had used the questioned path without trouble.

The process was lengthy and uncertain, and even the maps we used carried the formal disclaimer that the paths shown were not necessarily rights of way. Today the situation is very different. The 1949 legislation set out to define for all time which are the rights of way in the country, in such a way that their status could no longer be challenged. It required county councils, as the highway authorities for rural areas, to survey their territory and draw up a map, known as the definitive map, showing all the rights of way.

These rights of way were divided into three categories: footpaths that could be followed on foot only; bridleways for walkers and horse-riders, and now also for cyclists; and a rather unsatisfactory third form described as a 'road used as a public path', usually reduced to the unlovely abbreviation RUPP. This category ensured the inclusion on the definitive maps of the old roads, green lanes, etc, now used mainly for the same modest purposes as footpaths and bridleways.

31

Preparing the definitive maps entailed a great deal of work, and in many cases the field work of surveying and reporting on paths was taken on by volunteer parties of ramblers. This work, coupled with the need to provide for objections to be considered while maps were passing through their draft stages, meant that the original 5-year timetable was not adhered to. However, there are now definitive maps in existence for the whole of England with the exception of parts of Bedfordshire and Gloucestershire, and also for many former county boroughs, where the production of a map was an option rather than a duty.

The definitive map must be on public view in at least one office in each district and county, according to law. Some councils have also taken the commendable step of placing their maps in public libraries, which are of course open at hours more convenient to those working during the day. Most important of all is the decision of the Ordnance Survey to show the paths thus clearly defined in their legal status, with a distinctive marking on some of their more popular maps. One further point to know about the definitive maps is that they are required to be reviewed at regular intervals, when paths can be added or deleted. They are thus by no means a static record.

Having got the background clear, we really can answer the original question 'How can I be certain it is a right of way?' Firstly, if the map you are using is up-to-date, and your path is shown on it with the special marking, this is a clear indication that it appears on the county definitive map, or did when the map was published. If the county council has signposted the path, this is further positive evidence. But if there is still some dispute as to its status or the exact line it follows, your next move would be to check it on the definitive map itself; the county council will tell you where.

When you inspect the definitive map, remember that it is *conclusive* evidence that a right of way existed at the date the map was drawn up, and can even be used as such in court proceedings. It shows the rights of way drawn on an OS map of not less than 1:25000 scale, so there is no problem in locating the path precisely. Each path is identified by its own number, and there must be a statement accompanying the map to provide a description of the path. It is just possible that the path you are looking up, even when shown on the definitive map, may have been closed or diverted since the map was drawn up. If in doubt, ask the local council about this.

What is Trespass?

Having spent some time defining a right of way, it is very easy to worry over the consequences of straying from it. Of course you should do your best to keep to it, and follow the Country Code in every way; but if you *do* leave the path, then technically you are committing trespass. This is a civil rather than a criminal offence, and means simply that you are on someone else's property without authority. The landowner could sue you, but only for the damage you have caused. In many cases this would amount only to some bent blades of grass and damages would, to say the least, be minimal! For this reason the 'Trespassers will be Prosecuted' notices that still adorn the countryside really have little meaning, although if they are legitimately trying to warn you from straying on to private property, they should be obeyed.

Many farmers and landowners are not particularly concerned about trespass, provided you are clearly doing no harm. If you are challenged by one who *is* concerned, he can rightly insist that you leave his property by the shortest route to a public highway —possibly back on to the path you have strayed from. But, and a very important but, if you trespass *and* do real damage in the process, you could be prosecuted very effectively. If you make a thoughtless gap in a hedge, or a careless break in a fence, and thus allow valuable animals to stray, the cost to you could well be considerable. Occasionally you may find yourself on a path that is not a right of way, but which we use by the owner's permission. These permissive ways most often occur on private parkland or forest, and the owner may erect notices to state that he does not intend to dedicate his path as a right of way, or he may still follow the traditional practice of closing it or charging for its use on one specified day in the year. These are simply his ways of ensuring that the path does not become a right of way. On these paths, the usual rules about who should look after them and keep them clear of obstructions do not apply; they are not public highways.

Where Can I Roam Freely?

It is easy enough to accept that in enclosed farming areas you should keep carefully to the footpaths, but it is very tempting to think that on uncultivated land you can go where you please. This is very far from the case. There are certain areas where you have the *right* to roam freely, and others where you have no defined rights but where there is a long tradition of permissive access.

Areas where you have a right to access fall into two categories. First of these are areas covered by access agreements or orders made by the local authority under that excellent National Parks Act of 1949 mentioned earlier. This Act introduced for the first time the idea of negotiated access to 'open country' in return for compensation payable to the landowner. More than 35,000 hectares have now been opened to the public in this way, principally open moorland in the Peak District National Park, the scene of many bitter clashes between ramblers and gamekeepers in years gone by. The other category is that of common land open to the public. There is a widely held misconception that the typical uncultivated common is freely open to the public. This is not so, and in many cases access is by custom, not by right.

After all, the commons were originally the waste lands of villages, where local people or commoners exercised certain rights —to graze cattle perhaps, or gather wood or peat for fuel. Right of access was confined to commoners, and no general public right existed. There are various ways in which commons can formally be made available for public access and the Commons Society estimates that up to 150,000 hectares, or about a quarter of the total, are open to the public today. Unfortunately neither land covered by access agreements nor public access commons are clearly identified on our maps yet. It is a matter of guesswork and getting to know any such land in your area.

There are two major landowners who generally allow public

The notice attached to this signpost near Stockport refers to an application to divert the path, but eight houses have already been built across it, constituting a clear obstruction

access to their land—the Forestry Commission and the National Trust. Trust land, which includes some of our best loved areas of country, has long been shown on OS maps, and recently a policy has been adopted of showing Forestry Commission land as well. So our maps can guide us to some classes of open country; but note that open National Trust land does not include the many historic buildings in its care, where admission charges may apply not only to the house but also to the grounds around.

Can the Paths Change?

It can be very confusing to meet the suggestion that paths have been closed or moved from the line that the map shows. There are ways in which this can happen, but only by due legal process. If you meet someone who assures you 'that path hasn't been there

The summit plateau of Kinder Scout in the Derbyshire Peak District, where the public can now roam freely thanks to negotiated access agreements

for years', or 'it goes over that way now', he *may* be right. On the other hand, he may be assuming an authority that the private individual does not possess. The fact is that the farmer or land-owner has no power to move or to close a public right of way. The most he can do is to ask the local authority to consider doing this in his interests. If you are told that a path has been closed, check with the local authority to see whether an official order has been made.

This is the way it would be done, and the way in which you might become aware of the order at a time when you could have something to say about it. A notice is required to be placed at both ends of the length of path in question, to explain (sometimes in rather pedantic language) the effect of the order. It must also tell you where a copy of the order and plan can be inspected and where, and by when, objections to the proposal should be sent.

A similar notice must be published in the local paper. Anyone can object. You can object, local people can object. Perhaps there are local footpath conservationists keeping a special lookout for such cases, and they can object. If there is no objection, the authority confirms the order and advises when it will come into effect.

If there are objections, the matter is referred to the Department of the Environment, which arranges for an independent inspector to conduct an inquiry and make recommendations. On the evidence he hears he will decide for or against the order, and when the Department issues its decision, it is final. Only by such a process can a path be closed; it was decided as long ago as 1315 that a path cannot be lost merely because it has not been used. It follows, though, that recent use of a path may be an important factor considered by an inspector when conducting his inquiry as to whether or not a path is any longer needed for public use.

Who Maintains Paths?

Just as public footpaths and bridleways are as much highways in law as the motorways and trunk roads, so there are authorities with a responsibility for maintaining them. The highway authorities—county councils and London borough councils—are required to maintain all highways. In some counties the work is carried out by the district councils by arrangement, but the responsibility for seeing that the work is done remains with the county. The duty to maintain highways includes a duty to repair them where necessary. But what standard of maintenance should a humble footpath aspire to?

Back in 1950 a Ministry circular answered this in a sensible way, which ramblers would agree with. It said 'where paths are used mainly for pleasure by ramblers, it will no doubt generally be sufficient that they should be free from obstruction of impassable water or mud, that they should be inconspicuously but sufficiently signposted or marked where necessary. The main consideration is clearly that they should serve their purpose, whether business or pleasure, and not that they should conform to some arbitrary standard of construction'. Well put! 'Serving their purpose' can be taken to mean giving simple pleasure to folk using country paths, who would want no more than easy passage rather than asphalt under foot or other elaborate aids.

The term 'maintenance' has recently been defined by the courts as not including the removal of obstructions. However, there is a separate duty placed on highway authorities to 'prevent as far as possible the stopping up or obstruction of highways'. Despite this clear-cut duty, with parallel powers to take legal action or physically remove obstructions, the authorities are far too often reluctant to act. Barbed wire continues to cross a path where a stile should be. A builder plants a new house right on the line of a path, hoping thus to avoid the delays while a proper diversion proposal is being considered. These things *do* happen, and when you meet such a case it almost invariably means that an authority is not shouldering its responsibilities. Anyone is entitled to take out a private summons and prosecute someone who is obstructing a public path, and we owe a debt of gratitude to public-spirited people who have done this on our behalf. But be warned—apparently simple and straightforward cases may well have hidden complications, or fail on a minor technical point, with expensive consequences.

Paths and Access in Scotland

This chapter deals primarily with England and Wales, for Scotland has somewhat different concepts of public paths and access to open country. Walkers in the Highlands will find that they are allowed free access almost everywhere, except perhaps in the deer-stalking season from July to October. Your maps will show some footpaths and drove roads through the hills, but as Scotland has prepared no definitive maps, these routes cannot always be accepted as rights of way. There are other variations in the law; for example a public path can be closed after 40 years of disuse. Local *planning* authorities have a duty to keep public paths clear of obstructions, and they or other local authorities can take on their maintenance, signposting etc as well, but no statutory obligations are involved here. The bull situation is covered by national legislation in Scotland, and you may meet one of the safer breeds on a path, provided it is with cows or heifers.

The Obligations that go with Rights

When we walk in the country we expect our rights to be respected. But rights entail obligations, and we in turn need to be considerate of those whose land we cross, and to respect their livelihood. The Countryside Commission's Country Code provides a commonsense guide.

Guard against all risk of fire. As well as the more obvious sources of fire such as dropped matches or cigarette ends, pieces of broken glass have been known to cause fires in exceptionally dry weather.

Fasten all gates, unless you are certain that the farmer wants the gate open for his own purposes. One of the most common complaints by farmers about people in the countryside concerns the damage caused by cattle straying through gates left open.

Keep dogs under proper control, and if in doubt put the lead on. A dog used to town life often reacts quite differently when out in a field of sheep.

Keep to the paths over farm land. Remember that grass is a valuable crop, and on upland farms may be the only one.

Avoid damaging fences, hedges and walls. A broken wall or fence is not only expensive to repair, but also allows animals to roam. You should find a stile or gate if you are on a public right of way. If not, see Chapter 4 for advice on what to do.

Leave no litter. Litter is not only unsightly, it can be dangerous to animals or to other people.

Safeguard water supplies. Country properties may depend on a small stream or well for their drinking water. Do not pollute it.

Protect wild life, wild plants and trees. Leave them for others coming after you to enjoy.

Go carefully on country roads. The unexpected may be just round that blind corner, and unaware of you.

Respect the life of the countryside. A few thoughtless deeds by one person can sour attitudes and create friction for many who follow.

4 Problems You Could Meet

In popular walking country you can take many a footpath outing without ever meeting anything that could be described as a problem. If you are following a walk already planned out and described for you by someone else, you can be fairly sure that the author has been careful to avoid any difficult paths in favour of the ones he knows to be easy and clear. However, keeping to these well trodden ways will hardly lead you to a full appreciation of the wayward pleasures of our countryside, and before long you will be wanting to explore deeper, to try other tempting paths and less familiar parts. Then, you *will* meet problems, though hardly ever insurmountable ones, or serious enough to detract from the day's enjoyment. Rather they will be the kinds of hazard that only serve to remind us that the countryside is a living landscape where features change in the natural way of things; and Mother Nature herself can, given a few years' opportunity, spread herself abundantly over the line of our path.

You will be reminded, too, that the path leads through a land that has been farmed for many generations. Today's farmer, like his forefathers, continues to earn a living from the land, and it is hardly a cause for surprise if our path shows us evidence of that fact—the temporary fence across his grazing or the churned-up mud of his farmyard. The farmer, like other human beings, can on occasions be forgetful, or selfish, in going about his work. Then the problems you meet on the footpath will be man-made.

It is worth remembering, though, that the paths we follow have been part of that countryside for centuries. There are no fundamental reasons why today, as in the past, our simple use of the paths as a means of passage and the farmer's use of the same countryside to earn a living should not continue side by side. Many of the problems we meet today are, in fact, legacies of a period when the paths were under-used. Now, with better signposting and many more feet tramping out the line of a path over field and wood, nature has less chance of taking over, and

40

the farmer less excuse for absentmindedly fencing it across. Year by year it becomes easier to find and follow the paths, so do not be discouraged by our catalogue of problems. They are fewer than they used to be.

What To Do, Now and Later

There are two distinct questions you may have to answer when you come face to face with a footpath problem—how to get round it immediately, and what you are going to do about it later on. Some advice can be helpful on both points. Your immediate course of action will be guided by common sense and a knowledge of what the law entitles you to do. The possibility of doing something more, later on, is a point that may not always be obvious. But remember that others will be walking your path after you, meeting the same problem.

There are authorities responsible for seeing that hazards are removed, and many enthusiastic teams of footpath volunteers prepared to take up cases, pursue the authorities and, if need be, put in the work necessary to restore a path to good walking order. But neither party can do anything until someone alerts them that something is wrong. So it makes sense to know *who* is responsible for taking action in each area, *who* to inform, and also how far individuals can effectively go in tackling a case themselves.

Of course, some problems are too minor to be worth taking up—just the kinds of minor inconvenience you will expect in the countryside. Others are just as obviously temporary. But in cases where a formal approach or some downright hard work could put matters right, then other walkers will be deeply indebted to you if you take the problem up in the right quarters.

The trouble you are most likely to meet, comes under the broad heading of obstruction, either natural or man-made, and some definition is immediately necessary.

Just What Is Obstruction?

In everyday use the word 'obstruction' tends to mean something that makes passage impossible. If a house were built on the line of a footpath (and it *does* happen), this would be an obstruction in the total sense. But applied to highways, its definition is a lot wider, covering anything that makes our passage less easy than it used to be. Thus crops growing over the line of a path have been ruled to be an obstruction. They make it very much more difficult to walk than it used to be before the field was cropped over. A locked gate can also be an obstruction, even on a footpath, because it was obviously much easier to use the path when the gate could be opened. Even the humble stile is an obstruction, and although well built and sensibly proportioned ones are considered to be acceptable obstructions, an extra high stile where none had previously existed could well be unacceptable in law.

The responsibility for keeping paths free of obstruction is shared between the district council and the county council (acting as the highway authority). The county authority has the statutory responsibility for maintaining the path, and also deals with ploughing problems, stiles, gates and footbridges—matters that could be thought of as the 'structure' of the path. District councils have a general duty to look after public rights and to prevent 'as far as possible, the stopping up or obstruction of highways'. But, even at county level, do not expect fast or spectacular action. The sad fact is that footpath officer appointments are only a recent innovation, and even where they exist, they have neither staff nor funds to deal adequately with matters that arise over perhaps several thousand miles of rural paths in their county.

Now for a closer look at the obstructions you may meet.

The Fencing Problem

In theory any fence that crosses your path should have some means of easy passage through or over it. This is not always so, alas! But it should be remembered that simple fencing is seldom deliberately intended to keep walkers out; it is there to keep animals in. Even the simplest fence of barbed wire can be a vexatious obstruction, however, liable to snag your clothing whether you try to pass over, through or under it. In law you are entitled to remove as much of an obstruction like this as is necessary to get by, strictly on the line of the right of way, of course, and it has been suggested that this could mean cutting through the top two strands of a four-strand fence. In practice such adherence to legal entitlement could seriously weaken the fence; sheep and cattle could find their way through the gap, with potentially disastrous consequences for the farmer. There is also the risk of removing *more* of the obstruction than the law would deem necessary, leaving us open to a charge of malicious damage.

That leaves us still facing a barbed wire fence. Often the farmer's own solution (he too has to get around his fields) is to throw a piece of sacking over the barbs so that the points are largely protected, and he will carry his sacking around with him. Ramblers, who probably will not be so well equipped, might be able to follow his example by finding one of the plastic fertiliser bags often discarded by the farmer and left lying in the fields, to use it in the same way. If you want to go prepared for barbed wire, consider taking one or two short lengths cut from an old cycle tyre. Fit these over the barbs while you negotiate the fence, then remove them and take them with you, or leave them for the benefit of other ramblers who come to the same obstacle.

Far better than cutting your way through barbed wire, thereby bringing down the wrath of the farmer upon all ramblers present and future, is to report it as an obstruction to the county council. Then the landowner will be formally required, either by the county or by the district council acting as its agent, to remove the obstructing fence or insert a stile on the line of the path. If he persists in ignoring the request, the authority can finally carry out the necessary work themselves, and recover the costs from the landowner. It is easy enough to imagine the time such a process can take, but even so it is the right process because it makes the landowner aware of his obligations in a clear and fair way.

Electrified Fencing

Perhaps the greatest hazard of the single-strand electric cattle fence, often to be found on meadow paths, is its near invisibility. Even when ticking away menacingly, such fences are of low enough voltage not to cause humans any real distress, but on contact they can give a nasty jolt. Their use to subdivide fields for controlled grazing is strictly temporary, and at their usual 2ft 6in height from the ground they are not considered to constitute an obstruction. Considerate farmers will provide an insulating rubber surround on the wire at the point where a path crosses, which enables one either to step over the fence or detach it from its current source. Probably a stick is the most useful device for holding the bare wire down while a companion steps over, and he can do the same for you. If the process of raising or lowering the wire pulls any of the vertical stays out of the ground, they must of course be replaced, as must the wire should it be detached from the current.

The Other Boundaries

Hedgerows, and the drystone walls that often serve as field boundaries in the north and in limestone country such as the Cotswolds, are very much more permanent than mere wire fences. They do not spring up overnight—many have stood on the same line for centuries—and if your footpath crosses one, it will be unusual not to find due provision for crossing. The hedge should have gate or stile, and the stone walls steps, a squeeze stile, a gate or even sometimes a ladder stile. If there is no sign of such a crossing, first ask yourself whether you could have strayed from the path. If you are sure you are right, then proceed. Stone walls can be climbed by choosing a well built portion that has some long heavy stones projecting right through the thickness of the wall. Use these as steps, being careful not to dislodge stones or weaken the structure in any way.

Hedges cannot be tackled in the same way. A well maintained hedge is, like a fence, a containing field enclosure, and trying to force your way through could cause a gap big enough for cattle to use. You had better try to find an alternative way round, such as a distant gate that will lead you back to the path further on.

The Fastened Gate

It is not unusual to find a farm gate with a stile right beside it
to take the footpath right of way. In cases where there is no stile,
the gate should be openable. Farm workers have something in
common with old-time sailors when it comes to tying complex
knots in the rope that sometimes secures gates, but never forget
that they have good reasons for wanting to keep their gates
shut, even if their methods are sometimes crude. See that you
shut gates behind you, by whatever method, unless they are
obviously and deliberately fixed open for the convenience of the
farmer.

A gate that cannot be opened, either because it is padlocked or
securely wired up, is technically an obstruction. On a bridleway,
where horse-riders have a right of passage, this can be a very
serious matter, but on a footpath walkers will usually climb over,
grumbling the while. Whether such a case is worth taking up will
depend on how difficult the obstacle is, and whether its location
—for example, at the very start of a path—would deter some
users by suggesting that there was no right of way. If you do
climb a gate, climb it at the hinge end, where the gate will not
be unduly strained, even if you are.

Ploughed Paths and Growing Crops

Until fairly recently the farmer had no right to plough over the
paths and bridleways on his land, except in a few cases where
tradition accepted that it always had been ploughed in living
memory. But today, in recognition of his mechanised farming
methods, he has that right, and it is not uncommon to find your
path ploughed in spring, or under growing crop later in the year.
Unfortunately, too, many paths that once crossed open meadows
now cross fields that are cultivated every year; this is one of the
changes in farming practice that effects some counties more than
others.

When you find your path ploughed in this way, you are
naturally tempted to walk round the perimeter of the field rather
than tramp across it, particularly if the field is a small one pro-

vided with an uncultivated margin known as a headland, where you can comfortably walk. But where no margin has been left, the correct, if muddy, course is to stride out across the field, keeping as close as possible to the line of the right of way. Ramblers, with a reluctance to trample any land that the farmer has cultivated, may be loath to do this but, in fact, wherever a field has been ploughed from edge to edge, this course does the least damage. Walking round the boundary will mean walking a longer distance and thus trampling more of the field than if you keep to the straight line of the path. Remember, too, that if you leave the right of way, even with the good reason that the path is ploughed and difficult to walk, you run the risk of being warned off for being where you have no right to be.

If you do have to walk through growing crops, try to do no unnecessary damage. With a companion or party, keep to single file and stick to the line of the path as closely as you can. When you can see the exit on the far side of the field, this is easy enough. When it is in doubt, it makes sense to send one person from the party across first to find the exit, then to act as a more obvious marker for the others as they walk over.

In theory today the farmer should give his highway authority (ie the county council) at least a week's notice that he is going to plough up a footpath, which is, of course, a highway. He is then required to restore the surface of the path within 6 weeks. If he fails to give notice, he must restore it within 3 weeks of ploughing. These requirements may surprise the rambler familiar with ploughed paths, for in most cases the farmer does none of these things; neither is there any clear definition as to what is meant by 'restoring the surface'.

Probably the most practical way is for the farmer to drive his tractor up and down the line of the path immediately after ploughing. If this is done with the wheels overlapping on a centre line, it leaves a clear route across the field and we can then walk more easily on the flattened ground of the tractor tread marks than the ridges thrown up by the plough. Most important of all, it would redefine the line of the path, temporarily lost under the furrows. The Ramblers' Association has advocated this method, and now you will find some farmers using it.

But what of those that fail to restore footpaths? The county council can be approached, but so far local authorities have done little to see that this particular aspect of the law is complied with. Unlike other kinds of obstruction, this is one instance where the individual cannot act himself; action can only come from the highway authority, or the district or parish council. The highway authority can also restore a path with its own labour today, if the farmer has not done this himself within the required time limits. Then they can recover the costs from the reluctant farmer, probably a more effective persuasion than any other. There are two paths the farmer has still no right to plough at all: one is the 'headland path', the right of way that follows the boundary of the field, where a strip must be left for it; and the other is the green lane or byway with the official status of 'road used as a public path'.

The Overgrown Path

In a living countryside paths can quickly become overgrown if they are not frequently walked, and if no attempt is made to cut the vegetation back. As a problem it can vary from the nettles and brambles entwined around a stile to the green lane where blackthorn hedges have grown inward to cover the entire width in an impenetrable jungle. The first little vexation might well be dealt with by a few swipes with a stick, or some clipping with the secateurs you happen to be carrying in your pocket; but the path that is almost impassibly overgrown presents a very different problem, calling for sterner measures.

Although ramblers will naturally think of overgrowth as an obstruction just as everything else that makes his path more difficult to follow, it is officially regarded as a maintenance problem. There is in fact a division of responsibility, the highway authority having the duty to deal with surface growth on the path, and the landowner expected to restrain the overhanging vegetation of adjoining hedges and trees. So if you find your path obscured in this way, report it to the county council. But again, as they have so little labour available for such tasks as clearing country footpaths, do not expect fast action.

Results will probably come faster if you also contact a local footpaths group or the Ramblers' Association, which itself has 130 local groups engaged in footpath work. These path-preservation group range from ad hoc village societies set up to protect their own parish paths to major organisations based on nearby towns. Many organise volunteer working parties, armed with scythettes, ripsaws and loppers, to tackle badly overgrown paths. They see their efforts as a form of self-help, with the added satisfaction of knowing they are helping others to enjoy a country walk. You will seldom be aware that anyone has been at work on your path; their achievements are rather reflected in the absence of problems for you to struggle through. Sometimes they act as agents for the county council, which may even have provided the tools they use. Almost invariably they will be acting only with the willing consent of the landowner himself, who realises the benefits of an easy-to-follow path that people will not be tempted to stray from.

In case you find yourself taking part in an operation such as this, one word of caution. Our right to use a footpath does not entitle us to set out, individually or in an organised party, with the specific aim of clearing a path, or any similar task. For this you need permission.

The Path that Falls Away

A path that follows a river bank can be washed away. A cliff fall can carry away the path along its edge. In both cases, alas, the right of way goes with it! It would be comforting to think that the public path merely moves back when erosion occurs, but not so. The law insists that a right of way follows one defined line only, and if that line is left in mid air, the right of way effectively ceases to exist.

Of course, there are many cases where a landowner will raise no objection when the public do walk around a newly eroded area, and gradually the path will be established on a new line. But while this is happening, you could be turned back as a trespasser. The only remedy lies with the local authority, which can repair the bank and thus restore the path to its original line, or, alternatively, seek agreement with the landowner for the dedication of a new right of way.

The same situation occurs when a landslip blocks the line of your path. Again it is up to the local authority to remove the blockage or see that a new route is dedicated for public use.

Mud, Glorious Mud

It is the duty of the highway authority to keep paths in such repair as to be reasonably passable at all seasons of the year. But even this formal statement of responsibility has to take into account the nature of the path and who is going to be using it. No walker will be surprised to meet some mud on a remote country path, and plenty of it perhaps after winter snows have melted. He will not raise a plea for paving or asphalting. He will more likely make a mental note to take gumboots next time. It is only when a path is in a permanently waterlogged state that one can reasonably look to the highway authority to rectify matters, by drainage, resurfacing or even stepping stones.

Having covered the problems that obstruct the path, we must now look at a few of the other hazards you could encounter.

Bulls, and Others

Townsfolk have been known to be concerned for their safety when encountering any large four-legged creatures in the countryside. Horses, cows, and bullocks in particular can be inquisitive and frisky when walkers use the paths across their fields, rushing up to inspect the visitors. Hardly ever is there the slightest danger, for they usually keep their distance. Bulls are the only animals to watch out for, since they are intimidating and always potentially dangerous. They are usually easy to distinguish from cows and heifers by their size, nose ring and certain other items of equipment.

It has been suggested that certain breeds are more docile than others, and that a bull accompanied by cows is a less dangerous animal than one on its own, but there is no real evidence to support these surmises. The advice of experts at the Ministry of

Agriculture is that bulls should always be regarded as potentially dangerous, to be given a wide berth whenever possible. There is simply no such thing as a safe bull.

Are you likely to encounter a fully grown bull in fields crossed by footpaths? It can depend on which county you are in. In England and Wales the pasturing of bulls is generally controlled by local authority byelaws, approved by the Home Office, which itself recommends that no bull over 12 months old should be grazed in fields crossed by public paths. This is the restriction applied in most counties, but before the local government reorganisation in 1974 twelve counties had modified their byelaws to make them less stringent. Generally these modifications allow bulls to be grazed on public paths if accompanied by cows or heifers. This is the situation that still applies in the counties or former counties of Caernarvonshire, Cheshire, Denbighshire, Flintshire, Herefordshire, Holland and Lindsey in the county of Lincolnshire, Hunts and Peterborough, Isle of Wight, Kent, Merioneth and Oxfordshire. Two former counties, Brecon and Carmarthen, have no byelaws at all.

If you are within one of these old county boundaries, therefore, you *could* encounter a bull on your walk, under circumstances that some at least consider to be safe. Whether you consider it safe is a personal decision, but the best advice would seem to be to stay out of these fields, and most certainly do not enter them with dogs or children.

If you do happen to be halfway across the field before realising that it contains a bull, move quietly on, and, without losing sight of the bull, do nothing that might attract its attention. If the bull starts running towards you, then, and only then, run for the nearest field exit. Quoting the byelaws to it will seldom have any effect!

Unlike most footpath matters, the enforcement of byelaws is a job for the police. If you think the byelaws are not being observed, you can tell them, but it would be best to consult the district council first as to the nature and extent of byelaws in the area.

The only other animal likely to cause a walker concern is the farm dog. In general they are not dangerous; their prime purpose in life is to make a lot of noise when strangers are about, but they will turn and run when boldly faced. Against the snarling dog that seems keen to carry the matter further, the best defence is a stout stick, used with your booted feet to fend it off.

If you are unfortunate enough to be bitten, get proper medical treatment for the bite right away. Then report the matter to the police. An owner who allows a potentially vicious dog to be loose on a public path is clearly committing an offence; he may be trying to intimidate you from using the path and certainly others who walk the path after you are liable to depart with the same teeth-marks unless he is shown the consequences in law.

The Deterrent Notice

From bulls to 'Beware of the bull' notices is a logical step. While walking the paths, you may encounter notices that seem to be trying to dissuade you from using them, either by prophesying some dire fate, or by implying that the way is private. The signs with alarming messages such as 'Danger, fierce dogs' or 'Beware of the bull' are probably erected by owners who are deliberately trying to keep the public off their land. More often than not no such dangers lurk along the path; the sign is pure intimidation and nothing else. It follows that no creature thus acknowledged by the owner to be dangerous could be allowed access to a public way without the law being broken, a point that unfortunately we sometimes must put to the test by venturing along the path and facing its perils, nonexistent or otherwise. It is an offence for anyone to place notices like these on or near a public path, with intent to deter people from using it. An approach to the highway authority or district council will often see them removed.

The 'private' notice is a trickier problem, because, even when misleading, it can often be literally true. A private drive or track can quite legitimately carry the sign 'Private, no road' to deter use by vehicles, even though a public footpath follows it. A 'private' notice relating to woodland beside the path can easily be misinterpreted as applying to the path itself. 'Private' can even be seen on a farm gate, while a stile beside it marks the start of a public path. The farmer's field is private, the path is not. Where

51

this problem arises, the highway authority can usually be per-suaded to remedy it by erecting a public footpath sign alongside the notice to clarify the situation.

Bridges and Stiles

Footbridges are for the local authority to keep in good repair. They can range from a plank (or a railway sleeper) across a deep ditch to a lavish bridge across a sizeable river. It is not entirely unknown to find a bridge missing altogether; inadequate budgets mean long delays in getting such work done. As a result, volunteer path workers even turn out on occasions to build footbridges, supplying the labour and enthusiasm while the highway authority supplies the materials. But if you find a bridge missing or difficult to use in safety, report it to the county or district council.

Keeping stiles and gates in good order is the responsibility of the landowner. If approached, though, the local authority is obliged to contribute at least a quarter of the costs of repairs, and in some areas they do in fact cover all the costs or carry out the repair work themselves. If you meet problems with really difficult stiles, it would be worth notifying the local authority, so that it can take some action.

Those, then, are the problems. We have suggested lines of action you can follow up as an individual, but always remember that there are many dedicated voluntary societies that are striving to deal with these same problems in their own areas. They range from major regional bodies such as the Society of Sussex Downsmen, the Chiltern Society, or the Peak and Northern Footpaths Society, to small village path groups. Most will be experienced in knowing who to approach and how to get matters set right, and infinitely patient in pursuing path cases. They are good people to know, and you might even consider lending a hand in their work to keep the paths open. In any case, see that they hear about any problems you meet, with precise details and location (a grid reference if you can). The Ramblers' Association has a special obstruction report form you might find useful.

5 Finding Your Way

When you set out to take a country walk, you have three alternative ways of going about it. You can plan your own expedition, or follow a route that someone else has worked out and described for you, or join up with a party and leave the route-finding to an experienced leader. Beyond doubt the first way offers the most satisfying experience, but it can also seem daunting to beginners who will fear the possibility of getting lost. So most people will undoubtedly find their introduction to the countryside in one of the easier methods—the pages of a book of walks perhaps, or the programme of a rambling club.

However you set out, a good map should most certainly go with you. If you follow your own route, you will need this one essential guide to navigate by. Even following the instructions in a book of walks, you will find that a map tells you much more about the countryside around you, and of course will be ready to help if you should happen to wander from the described route.

Which are the right maps for walkers? They must show all the paths we want to use accurately, and give the landmarks that will help us locate them. Some maps will not show paths, because footpath walking is not what they are intended for, or because their scale does not allow such fine detail to be recorded. Others, by contrast, can show great detail but cover such a small area of countryside that even a modest outing will walk right off their edge, and force us to carry several sheets around with us. Somewhere between the extremes are the maps we need, but before making a choice it would be best to explain some of the technicalities.

Map Scales and Other Factors

A map, *any* map, is simply a reduction of features on the ground, to a size that allows them to be represented on a sheet of paper that can be folded and slipped into your jacket pocket or the glove compartment of a car. The scale of a map is the extent to which lengths on the ground have been reduced on it. A map can be drawn to any scale that suits its purpose. Until very recently we chose, for convenience, to work in miles and inches, but now with metrication many maps are using scales such as 1 : 50,000, which means for example that 1km on the ground is represented by just 1 fifty-thousandth of a kilometre on the map. Those who have mastered metric measures will be able to work this out to be 2cm.

The *longer* the length on the map that represents a particular distance on the ground, the *larger* the scale is said to be. The terms large-scale and small-scale are so often used in describing maps that this definition is important to get clear. A map drawn on 1 : 5,000 scale represents 1km on the ground as 20cm on the map, and is thus a larger scale than our 1 : 50,000 map. Perhaps the easiest way of keeping this clear in the mind is to remember that on a large-scale map every detail is shown larger.

In general, maps with scales of 1 : 25,000 or about $2\frac{1}{2}$in to 1 mile, or less, are referred to as small-scale maps, whereas the others are called large-scale. The scale of a map will be chosen according to how much detail it needs to show and how wide an area it should cover for convenience. Thus a long-distance car journey will call for very little map detail beyond the major roads, and the distance between starting point and destination can be well over 100 miles. So the motorist's route-planning map will normally be on a scale of about 1 : 625,000 or 1in to 10 miles. Surveyors and town planners, on the other hand, will use large-scale maps of 1 : 5,000 or 1 : 2,500, which even show the boundaries between house properties.

As footpath walkers, our needs are best met by maps at the scales of 1 : 50,000 or 1 : 25,000. Maps of smaller scale do not contain sufficient information about the country we are walking in—they do not, for example show all the footpaths. Maps of larger scale probably show too much detail, and cover too small an area of ground. Cyclists find the 1 : 100,000 scale very practical for their needs, and it would be adequate for planning a walk when you intend to stick entirely to lanes and tracks.

The range of landscape features shown on the map is obviously

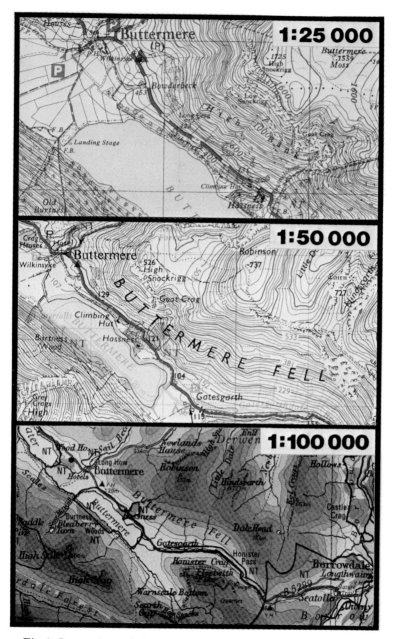

Fig 2 Comparison of three map scales of the same Lake District area (Top two maps: Crown Copyright reserved)

another big consideration for the walker. The typical road map tells us virtually nothing of the countryside we drive through, but once we park and start a footpath walk, we need to have plenty of information to guide us. Features on the ground will be represented on the map by symbols of various kinds, usually explained in a key. Of course the larger the map's scale, the more detail it will have room for and the more symbols we can expect to find. As country-goers we shall need to have the public paths, lanes and tracks adequately depicted; also other features, the contours that show us the shape of the land, the woods, coppices, lakes and streams that form the major landmarks, and the farms, villages, even the humble 'PH' or public house that could be the objective of the walk. All these appear on maps of 1:50,000 scale and larger.

The accuracy of a map is one other factor to consider. In the true sense accuracy must depend on scale; none of our small-scale maps show every feature exactly as it is on the ground. Roads are shown wider than they really are, and the church or mill is nowhere near as big, or even the same shape, as the conventional symbol that represents it. But this minor inaccuracy is acceptable, for it does not effect our use of the map; rather it makes the map clearer to read. Inaccuracy due to careless drawing is not likely to bother us, at least in the UK. Our OS maps are generally as accurate as their scale allows. But the countryside is changing constantly, woodland areas may be extended or felled, new housing or roads spring up, so it makes good sense always to walk with the most up-to-date map available. An OS map will always have a note of its date of compilation and when revisions were made to it.

Now, having gained an idea of the scale and detail we need for a walking map, is it time to look at the map series available.

Ordnance Survey Maps

For walking in Britain the 1:50,000 and 1:25,000 scale maps of the Ordnance Survey, the government-sponsored map surveying and publishing agency, best meet the criteria we have set. In all 204 maps in the 1:50,000 scale cover England, Scotland and

Wales, each sheet spanning 1,600sq km. This scale of approximately 1¼in to the mile replaces the old 1in to 1 mile, but the maps are similar in many respects. They are maps much loved by countrygoers, with a subtlety of colour and tone in the representation of woodland and other landscape features that attempts to give a true 'picture' of the countryside and its character. The definitive footpath and bridleway rights of way are shown with a special red marking, except for a few limited areas where, sadly, this information is not yet available. They show other paths, too, which may not necessarily be rights of way. Contours are shown at 50ft intervals, although their height is now given in metres above sea level. Their wide range of symbols covers almost all the features we are likely to meet in the country, from the ancient tumuli and triangulation pillar on the hilltop to the windpump down in the valley or the disfiguring pylon line that, even so, provides another landmark to navigate by.

Most of the 1:50,000 scale maps at present available belong to what is known as the First Series. As a first stage in the process of metrication to the new scale, this series was photographically enlarged from the 1in maps it replaced, and thus shows almost exactly the same details, rather larger and therefore clearer. All heights above sea level were converted from feet to metres as part of the process.

Now an increasing number are appearing as Second Series maps, redrawn with some significant changes aimed at making the maps even clearer in detail, so that more information for tourists can be included. Now country parks and open beauty spots, picnic sites, viewpoints and information centres appear on the map, but unfortunately some details that were valuable to walkers have been left off in the process. The distinction between deciduous and coniferous forest, which told many ramblers whether woods would be pleasant to stroll in or not, has been dropped, as has the symbol for bracken, heath and rough grassland. On the credit side the Ordnance Survey has agreed to a suggestion from the Ramblers' Association that Forestry Commission land be identified on these maps. As the Commission allow free access to most of their forests, this information will be very valuable to walkers when added.

Of greatest importance to the rambler are of course the foot-paths themselves. On the First Series maps they are represented in definitive form as a line of fine red dots, all too easily obscured by other detail and none too easy to see clearly, as many users have discovered. On Second Series maps this marking is replaced by a more confident red 'pecked' line, so on balance you should find the latest maps easier to read.

Suitable and attractive though the 1:50,000 scale maps are, some people prefer to use the 1:25,000 maps when walking, particularly in intricate countryside, because of the even greater clarity and detail afforded by the larger scale. The most significant extra detail provided by these maps is the field boundaries —the lines of walls and hedges that are extremely valuable when tracing the line of a footpath over enclosed country.

Again by way of complication, there are two series to contend with on this 1:25,000 scale. The First Series covers England and Wales, with rather inconveniently small sheets spanning 100sq km each. The Second Series, which is gradually replacing the First, covers 200sq km with each sheet, giving more up-to-date information. This series also offers the supreme advantage of showing the rights of way with a special definitive marking, and is thus a much more attractive buy for walkers. Unfortunately it has not been published en bloc, and sheets are appearing at the rate of approximately eighty per year. If you are lucky enough to be walking in an area for which this superior Second Series map has been published, then go out and buy it. It is one of the world's finest small-scale maps.

Maps for the Most Popular Areas

Apart from these 1:50,000 and 1:25,000 scale series that aim to span the entire country, the Ordnance Survey also publishes a number of special maps on similar scales for some of the most popular touring areas. Their latest development, the 1:25,000 Outdoor Leisure Series, is proving very popular. Areas so far covered include the Dark Peak (Northern Peak District of Derbyshire), the Three Peaks (Limestone country of Ingleborough, Whernside and Penyghent), the English Lakes (in four separate sheets), the Brecon Beacons (East, Central and West), and the Brighton and Sussex Vale. They cover about 600sq km each, and show rights of way, open access areas, viewpoints and a wealth of extra information of value to walkers.

Tourist maps are also available, still usually on the old 1in to 1 mile scale, for such popular areas as the Lake District, North Yorks Moors, New Forest, Exmoor and Dartmoor. These maps give such extra information as car parks, information centres, camping sites etc, but their outstanding feature is the use of colour-tinted layers and shading to supplement the contour lines. This makes the relief stand out more clearly, adding an extra dimension that is particularly useful when planning a walk in hill country.

The Ordnance Survey publishes a catalogue setting out all its current publications and the names and addresses of its main dealers. Most booksellers will have some of the 1:50,000 maps in stock, and many also stock Outdoor Leisure, Tourist and local 1:25,000 sheets.

Only one other national map series is of interest to walkers in this country, the maps published by Bartholomew's at a scale of 1:100,000, a new version of a series known for many years as the $\frac{1}{2}$ in to 1 mile scale. These maps cover England, Scotland and Wales in sixty-two sheets. With their colour-tinted contours, they are useful for route planning or for planning a holiday, but detail is not sufficient for use when walking and only a very small proportion of footpaths are shown at all.

Signs and Waymarks

As well as the map you carry, there are certain aids in the countryside itself today to help you find and follow the path. At the point where your path starts you may find a signpost pointing in its general direction, reassuring you that it is indeed a public footpath or bridleway and perhaps also stating where the path leads and how far it is. But by no means all the paths are identified in this way. Do not be put off if your path is not signposted; this is no indication that it is not a right of way, only that the authority has not got round to providing a sign yet.

Local authorities have had a statutory duty to put up these signs wherever a footpath or bridleway starts off from a metalled road ever since the passing of the Countryside Act in 1968. Unfortunately no timetable was set down, and some counties lag far behind others. This is why some paths are still not signposted. Some forward-looking authorities, however, were signposting their paths for many years before the duty was imposed on them. The stubby wooden signs erected by Essex County Council as long ago as the 1930s are a fine example, and sturdy specimens can still on occasions be found pointing over the Essex fields.

But most signposting you meet today will have been carried out in the years since 1968, usually with a green and white metal pointer, small relation of a familiar family of road signs, or a shorter oak finger post. The information they offer is far from standardised, but it should give destination and distance in miles or kilometres and the status of the way—for instance, 'Public Footpath Moreton Mill 1.5km'. Occasionally symbols are used, a footpath in Gloucestershire being indicated by a walking figure, or by a stile symbol in Berkshire. Both wood and metal types are rather easily vandalised, by uprooting or by the humourist who turns them so that they no longer point the right way. Both types are also relatively expensive, but a major cost is undoubtedly the labour needed to take them out and place them. This is why, on occasions, teams of volunteer path enthusiasts may be called in to erect signs, particularly when the initiative for providing them comes from the local parish council.

Another economy measure you may occasionally meet is the use of sign-stones—little concrete blocks disturbingly like tomb-stones, set in the grass with 'Public Footpath' and destination moulded into their faces. In long summer undergrowth they can be difficult to find, except by tripping over them.

A signpost pointing the way at the start of a path will seldom be sufficient guide to its line further on, and the aid you will occasionally meet along the path is known as waymarking. Alas, waymarking is scarce over the countryside as a whole. It is mainly confined to those areas where active local path volunteers have provided it, or where a statutory body has taken a special

Painting a waymark on a Berkshire path. The white arrow follows the Ramblers' Association style used extensively in the Chilterns and elsewhere

61

interest, as in some of the National Parks or in the forests owned by the Forestry Commission. The waymark you are most likely to meet is the painted arrow, on a tree, stile or gatepost. In the Chiltern Hills the white arrows will have been painted by the Chiltern Society; in the Forest of Dean the yellow arrows have been provided, as on many Cotswold paths, by the local Ramblers' Association. Wherever the path turns or divides, the arrows will be there to direct you—pointing straight up for straight on, or angling to left or right to give you the new direction, just like the convention of the road sign.

These pioneering schemes have now, in a sense, been made 'official' by the publication of a recommended waymarking system by the Countryside Commission. This you will now begin to meet on country paths; the arrows look rather different from those we have mentioned, with a less defined head, and a colour coding identifies footpaths with yellow arrows and bridleways with blue. You will also currently meet many variations on the waymark theme, according to who has provided them. Sometimes only a non-directional blob of paint will identify the path, so that

Fig 3 The current Countryside Commission waymarking system

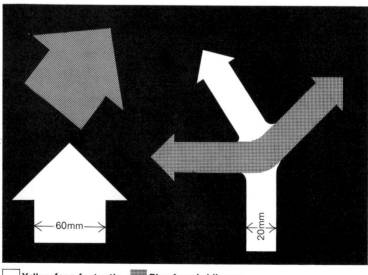

Yellow for a footpath   Blue for a bridleway

you will have to search ahead for the next blob before being sure of the line to follow. Local authorities will occasionally use small signs either carrying an arrow or the word 'Footpath', or both. Forestry paths have even been waymarked with an appropriate stencilled footprint. Even when obviously provided by keen amateurs, these waymarks can usually be relied on to define the path; the people who put them there will know their local paths intimately and the landowner has in most cases readily agreed to the work, knowing that a guide for ramblers along the path will ensure they never wander and trespass.

But remember, if your path *is* waymarked you are fortunate; so far very few are.

Planning a Walk

Your starting point will depend on your mode of transport into the country. Using rural buses or the country railway stations still open may restrict your choice of area somewhat, but with careful study of timetables you can plan a linear route, starting at one point and ending at another perhaps on the same line. This way you see more varied country and have that satisfying feeling of having linked distant points on foot. Using a car, your walk has to be a circular one, unless you park at or near a station and use the train to get back to it. Parking in fact can be a problem. Ideal spots to begin a ramble deep in the country will be the car parks provided at National Trust open spaces, at Country Parks and near many other beauty spots by National Park authorities and others.

In working out your route in advance it is best, particularly in the early stages, to underestimate your ability to cover distance. On a fine day, over easy ground, you may well feel like walking a lot further than you expected to, but it is much easier to extend a walk when you are in an energentic mood than to shorten one you are committed to. On fairly level walking most people will average from $2\frac{1}{2}$ to 3mph, but before trying anything ambitious find out what is your own comfortable walking pace. The true length of a walk is by no means just the distance on the map. In hill country the climbing, descending and rough going generally can extend the time needed for a walk very considerably. Even in lowlands the ground conditions will make a big difference according to the season. Walking along muddy tracks or across a ploughed field or two in winter can double the time needed for the distance and use up a lot more energy, not to mention the delays in scraping mud from boots. Coupled with the early approach of sunset, this can easily lead to the badly planned winter ramble ending in chilly darkness. In summer, too, a densely overgrown path can slow you down just as much. So unless you know a walk well already, allow time for the delays you have not planned for—which could occasionally include losing your way.

Which paths will be the easiest to find? Regrettably the map cannot tell you this; the fact that it shows a public footpath is no guarantee that there will be visible signs of the path on the ground. In popular walking country nearly all the paths will be at least faintly visible owing to regular use. A footpath that follows a clear feature like a hill-crest, the edge of a wood or a farm track will usually be easier to trace than a cross-country path, and a bridleway will probably be more conspicuous than a footpath, particularly in woodland, where riders will have kept it wider and higher. But even a bridleway can be ploughed out in open fields, so this is no infallible rule.

The Footpath Guides

It is an indication of the growing popularity of country walking that recent years have seen a multitude of local guides and maps appear for the path user. Many of these are prepared and published by footpath and amenity societies, or even by individual enthusiasts, making it impossible to give more than a general picture of the nature and range of material available, by selecting a few examples.

Most ambitious are the several major series of walking guides of regional significance. In the south London Transport, even in pre-war years, were publishing an excellent series of books on country walks around London. The latest versions maintain the high standard, the walks carefully chosen, the route descriptions concise, and the maps clear. Unfortunately they are only sold through ticket offices. But other publishers have followed where London Transport has led. The most extensive series, from Spurbooks, covers not only the country around London but areas all over Southern England: Dorset, the New Forest, the South Downs, etc.

Further north, and in a class and style of its own, is the series of books by A. Wainwright covering the Lake District and other walking areas in meticulous and affectionate detail. This famous series, which replaces the conventional printers' typesetting with script, maps and illustrations all from Wainwright's own hand, is regarded as indispensable by a whole generation of Lakeland lovers who walk his carefully delineated routes and take inspiration from his philosophy. Fortunately these books, published by the *Westmorland Gazette,* are available in good bookshops throughout the country.

It is not unusual for a series of walks to appear week by week in a local newspaper. Having attracted a regular following, they then appear as a collection in booklet form. These are among the most popular guides available: for example, the *Lancashire Evening Post* has published a book of walks around Preston, all of which appeared originally in the pages of the paper. Many other examples could be quoted. The *Kentish Times* has published a book of walks through Kent by V. W. Morecroft, who writes regularly for it. The *Surrey Advertiser* does likewise with walks from its own contributor, Geoffrey Hollis.

Another useful source of information is the guides and maps published by such official agencies with an interest in encouraging country recreation as the National Park Authorities, Tourist Boards etc. The Welsh Tourist Board, for example, has published a commendably comprehensive booklet on walking in Wales, which describes no less than 150 walks. In Devon the County Tourist Office publishes a series of leaflets on the waymarked paths over Dartmoor, and even the Western National Omnibus Company has had the initiative to publish free leaflets on walks in the county, based on their bus services, of course. In the Yorkshire Dales, the National Park Authority has published a series of leaflets on walking in the best known dales—Wharfedale, Wensleydale and others.

The many other maps and guides produced by local enthusiasts rather than commercial interests are unfortunately difficult to find, as distribution, handled by the same keen amateurs, is limited to the retail outlets they can persuade to stock them. Even so, some excellent material comes in this category. One valuable item is the local footpath map. This, unlike the conventional map, gives extra prominence to the footpaths and bridleways, often with their parish path number added as reassurance that they are all rights of way. A most striking example is the series of Ramblers' Maps of the Cotswolds prepared by the Gloucestershire Area of the Ramblers' Association, which are redrawn versions of the OS 1:25,000 scale maps with the footpath rights of way and other useful information added. The series of specially drawn footpath maps prepared by the Chiltern Society have also set a standard in their own way. They each take an intimate corner of the Chilterns, and define all the paths very clearly, with viewpoints, bus routes, bus stops and car parks—all the information a walker needs. Several of the best walks are described on the back.

Local path booklets have proved very popular, too, especially when written with family parties in mind. The success of such guides as *Park Your Car and Take a Walk*, prepared by the Furness (Cumbria) Ramblers' Group, testifies to this. Yorkshire is particularly well served by such local guides, including the well illustrated *Walking in East Yorkshire* by Dr G. R. Eastwood; *Walks around Harrogate* and *Footpaths of Leeds* by the two Ramblers' Groups in those areas. All these and many more are well worth finding in local bookshops.

The only comprehensive lists of local guides available are the Fact Sheets on Guides to Local Walking, obtainable from the Ramblers' Association. There are eight of these: South East, London, East Anglia, East Midlands, West Midlands and Wales, South West, North East, and North West. Specify which you want and enclose a large addressed envelope and 22p postage.

Following Someone Else

There is one further way of walking in the country—joining a party. It could be that on occasions you will enjoy, or even prefer, to walk with an organised group, for the pleasantly informal social contacts made and the relaxation of taking your ramble behind a leader who has very likely surveyed the route already. There is ample opportunity for you to do this. There are nearly 500 rambling clubs and societies affiliated to the Ramblers' Association, and very few parts of the country without a rambling group of some kind. Many will be independent local organisations, but the number also includes local groups of the Ramblers' Association, the Holiday Fellowship and the Youth Hostels Association, the last-named, of course, having an interest in hostel weekends as well as rambles.

Rambling clubs will vary in the age groups they appeal to, and in the strenuousness of their walks, but the majority attract a very wide range of ages, even to whole families. A typical pro-

An informal rambling party. Members of a Ramblers' Association local group exploring the paths of West Essex

gramme will have organised walks on Sundays throughout the year, but occasionally a club will find other days of the week popular. From the major cities public transport continues to be the basis of the club's rambling programme, but in smaller centres it is not unusual to find members using their cars to get to an agreed starting point, sharing accommodation when need be to see that nobody is left behind. Your public library will very likely hold information on local organisations, including rambling clubs, or, failing that, the Ramblers' Association can offer advice. Then a letter to the club secretary, with stamped addressed envelope, will usually bring their current programme and a cordial invitation to come and meet them on their next walk.

The club ramble will be a small informal affair. To cater for the heavier demand in major cities such as London, Manchester or Newcastle, more ambitious excursions are organised by train or coach, by the Ramblers' Association and others. As early as 1932 ramblers' excursions began running from London, and the tradition continues. On one Sunday each month the excursion uses coaches; on the other Sundays the ramblers use trains on Southern Region or the other British Rail regions. The coach excursions visit many areas of countryside that can no longer conveniently be reached by train. All these facilities are open to the public, fares are reasonable, and a choice of walks is offered from 10 to 12 miles in length, led by experienced volunteer leaders. They provide a good introduction to country walking, and an opportunity to meet a wide variety of fellow walkers. Information should be available from stations or from the Ramblers' Association.

Even if you contemplate a longer spell in the country—a walking holiday or weekend—there are many centres where you can enjoy the company of other ramblers. Guest houses run by the Holiday Fellowship, the Countrywide Holidays Association

An organised excursion. A party from a Southern Region ramblers' excursion train being led along a woodland walk

overleaf: Many Youth Hostels are superbly situated for walking. Coniston Coppermines hostel in the Lake District has been converted from the old mine manager's office – walks start from the door

and the Ramblers' Association in the Lake District and other attractive areas, specialise in walking holidays. Usually a resident leader will be there to lead parties on walks of several grades of strenuousness.

In addition over 250 hostels of the Youth Hostels Association in England and Wales are often situated deep in the very finest walking country. They range from simple mountain huts to well provided and comfortable superior-grade hostels and, it is important to stress, they are open to all ages from 5 upward, with no top limit. Some fifteen hostels even have special family accommodation. Children often prefer the friendly informal air of staying in a hostel, even the novelty of helping with the work and sleeping in bunk beds. You can use your car, too, to reach the hostel, provided you come with the aim of walking when you get there.

6 Following the Map

A map is simply a very accurate plan of the countryside. So the first stage in learning to navigate with a map is to try relating it to the area of country it represents.

Begin by familiarising yourself with the map symbols. Most important are the contours, which show you the shape of the land, and then those ways in which various types of vegetation and water feature are depicted. The streams, ponds and woods of the countryside are often the most visually prominent items, and we shall be using them soon to navigate by.

Fig 4 The basic contour patterns in hill country

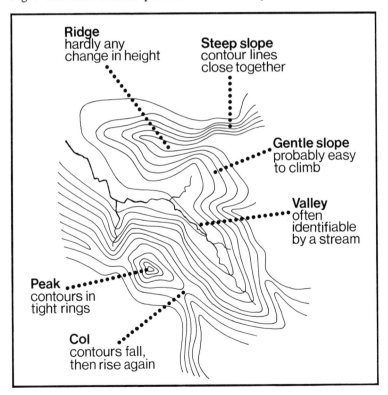

Contour patterns are very important and it is worth spending some time getting to recognise the forms that turn up most frequently (Fig 4). An understanding of contours is valuable for two good reasons. In route planning, particularly in hill country, the walker will usually want to find his way to the ridges and peaks by an 'economical' line—one that does not waste his energy on unnecessary climbs and descents. He may also need to pin-

Map and compass practice for ramblers on a YHA mountain-craft holiday in Snowdonia. Their fine viewpoint is Mynydd Cribau

point the passes linking adjacent valleys that will provide a lower and easier route over, avoiding dangerous summits and steep escarpments perhaps.

In lowland and upland country alike the relating of contour patterns on the map with the hills, slopes, valleys etc of the countryside you are walking over is just one of the ways you navigate accurately. If, for example, you find yourself faced with a choice of two paths, one falling and the other remaining level, contour lines alone can tell you which path you want to follow.

Trying it Out in the Field

Having familiarised yourself with the map symbols, your best way of relating the map to the countryside itself is by setting yourself a few simple exercises in the field. Take a 1 : 50,000 scale map up to a viewpoint that can be very easily identified on the map. Now set out the map in front of you and pick out a few point features on it—churches, isolated buildings, radio masts or anything else that is likely to show up prominently in the view before you. Then orientate the map so that imaginary lines drawn on the map from your viewpoint to the symbols you have chosen coincide with the direction of your own line of vision to the features in the landscape.

Next, try identifying on the map some of the other types of feature in the country around you. Follow the course of a country lane as it winds from one village to another. Pick out the route of a railway line or an overhead electricity transmission line and trace how these are marked on the map. Follow the outline of a lake or a wooded area and see how these also relate to the map (Fig 5).

If the land around you is fairly flat, you should find it easy enough to 'read' the map. The only distorting factor will be that of perspective. As long as you remember that the map is, in effect, a view of the country from directly above, while your view is a very oblique one, you should be able with a little practice to adjust for this distortion. A square block of woodland on the map will obviously appear to narrow away towards its far end as you

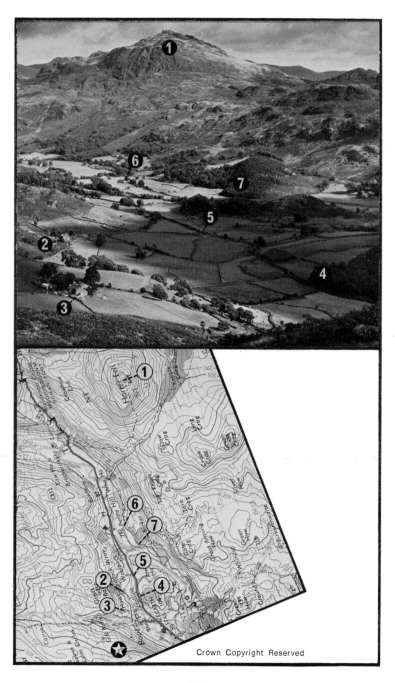

76

see it, because of this perspective effect. A lane may not take quite the angle you expected, until you make this adjustment.

A more awkward distortion of this kind of feature happens when the landscape is hilly or mountainous rather than flat. That block of woodland marked as a green square on the map may look anything but square if it lies on a steep hillside shaped by streams into valleys and spurs. Only practice in using maps over many types of terrain can make you expert in interpreting this level of distortion, but the key question to ask always is—how would that feature over there look from high and directly overhead? What would its shape be if I projected it up on to a horizontal plane and reduced it in scale? This is how features are represented on the map.

Another important exercise is relating contour patterns to the lie of the land around. It is obviously best to try this in hill country, where it is easy to identify summits, valleys, ridges and cols, and to see how they are shown on the map. Later on, move to other viewpoints and try to orientate the map solely from the form of the land around and the contour patterns on the map. Then check the map's orientation by locating any available linear and point features. If you are successful with exercises of this kind, you are beginning to gain proficiency in map reading. It is time then to move on to the next stage—map navigation.

Following Your Route with Map Only

If the map you are using is detailed enough, and if the country you are exploring offers sufficient features to navigate by, it is perfectly possible to follow the route of a walk by map alone. A compass can be helpful, and in some kinds of country it becomes essential, as you will read later, but it is well worth knowing how to find your way by map alone before learning how to use a compass as well.

Fig 5 The map is orientated on a prominent peak (1). Two nearby farms are easy to identify (2 and 3) while an equally prominent wood (4) helps to locate the winding valley road (5). The more distant Penny Hill Farm can then be found (6) along its own lane. Distant woodland on the sloping hillside (7) relates well to the map

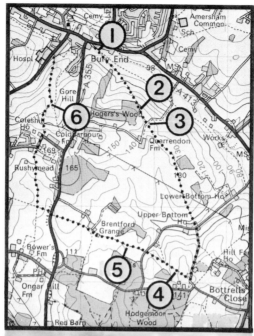

Fig 6 A typical short walk in the Chilterns, illustrating a few of the situations met when navigating public footpaths by map

1 Two paths start from the gate. One stays level but our path climbs to pass just below the first belt of trees, then crosses the corner of a second belt, already visible beyond the first

2 As the path emerges from the second belt of woodland, we find that Quarrendon Farm is hidden from view by a curve of hillside. However, the right hand corner of a distant coppice is our aiming point, visible over the brow of the hill

3 Now in the open again with further stiles to guide us, the line of the path can be related to two coppices. It follows a hedge to the corner of the first, then bears right, away from the second

4 A good viewpoint, and the buildings of Brentford Grange can be seen almost a mile ahead. This aiming point gives us the immediate line of our path over open pasture, as it heads almost straight for the Grange

5 Nearer to Brentford Grange the farm buildings come into view again, and we know our path will pass near them. Stiles in the field boundaries confirm the line

6 Problem spot. Our path has been ploughed and its line no longer visible. But contours give one clue – the path crosses the shoulder of a gentle ridge. The distant church tower gives us another – the path heads a few degrees to the left of it

Once again, it is much easier and more fun to master the art of map navigation by practical exercises than by any armchair method. There is just one important principle to apply all the time: when travelling across country, it is important *always* to know your position on the map as accurately as possible.

Take a 1:50,000 series map—Second Series if you can get it —of a lowland area and plan out a short circular walk of 3 to 5 miles (Fig 6). At the starting point orientate the map and identify the shape of the country that you are going to walk through. Look for some of its more prominent features—churches, rivers, woods, a village perhaps—which can help you keep a sense of direction.

Now see which nearby features are going to help you follow the line of the footpath—a building it passes by perhaps, or the corner of a wood that it touches. As you begin your walk, other features come into view. Keep aware of your position on the map as you move along, and think ahead to visualise how the route will continue in relation to the new landmarks. It will surprise you as you get used to the process how even the simplest of English lowland landscapes will almost always provide several 'reference points' that enable you to judge your position.

When you come to a point that can clearly be identified on the map, check time and distance. On this first leg of the journey you should quickly become familiar with the scale of the map. On level ground a normal walking pace will be about 1 mile in every 20 minutes—about 1in on a 1:25,000 map for every 8 minutes walking.

Public footpaths do not always follow such convenient linear features as hedges or tracks, and you will soon find yourself having to navigate from point to point without an obvious line to guide you. Try following the line of a footpath from one side of a field to another, or even across several fields in succession. If the path is well trodden, this will still be easy, but if it is not, the map must be carefully orientated at the start of the footpath, the angle judged and your position checked against surrounding features at frequent intervals along the path to ensure that you do not wander far from the true route. Often on a cross-country walk like this the accuracy of your navigation will be confirmed every so often by the discovery of a stile in the field boundary almost exactly where you expected it to be—a very satisfactory feeling!

Obviously it is only practical to navigate in this way without a compass over enclosed country with very little featureless ground to cross. Even in enclosed country a walk with a 1 : 50,000 scale map alone can pose problems, because these maps do not show field boundaries as the 1 : 25,000 maps do. A hedge can be a useful aid to navigation, and when the path follows it, there is some advantage in knowing which side of the hedge it is on. The 1 : 25,000 map will tell you. However, a knowledge of how to use a compass is always useful and sometimes essential—so this is the next technique to acquire.

Using Map and Compass

Everyone knows that a compass is a device for showing the direc-

Fig 7 A simple compass exercise

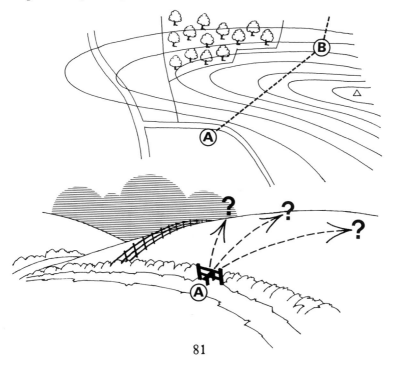

tion of magnetic north, but many people are at a loss to understand how a compass is used along with a map, and how the two are used together in finding a route across the countryside. When you have tried out map navigation over a variety of different types of country, you will readily appreciate the value of a compass. When the number of identifiable points becomes small; when the ground to be crossed is wide, open and featureless; and, worst of all, when mist or fog descends; then a map alone is insufficient. You may know exactly where you are and the route you want to follow on the map. But which direction do you start walking in, and how do you stick to it? By using the compass.

Consider the simple and typical little navigation exercise of Fig 7. You have reached the stile into open country at point A and you want to follow the right of way, not marked in any form on the ground, across the shoulder of the hill to point B. Because of the hill point B is not visible to you, although you can clearly identify it on the map. If you go too far to the right, you will be climbing higher than necessary, if you wander too far leftwards,

Fig 8 A typical Silva compass

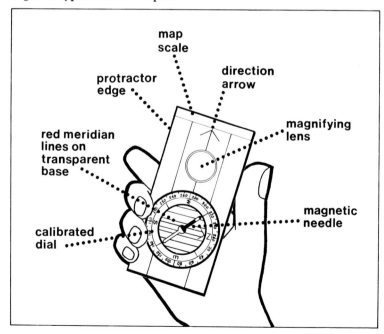

this will lead you into the woods on the other side of the hill.

A theoretical way of finding the route would be as follows. Draw a straight line on the map between A and B. Measure the angle between grid north (indicated on the map by the north-south grid lines) and the line A–B. Make an adjustment to this angle to allow for the fact that the compass will point to magnetic north and not grid north. Then take up the compass, turn it so that the needle points to the north point on the compass casing, find the direction passing through the angle calculated from the map and follow it across to point B.

With a conventional protractor and compass this exercise could be done accurately but slowly. With a modern compass such as the Silva model shown in Fig 8, all these steps can be carried out faster and with very little effort. This is because the Silva compass can be used both as protractor and magnetic direction finder. With it, the above exercise proceeds as follows. Place the edge of the compass on the map between A and B, with the direction arrow pointing in the general direction A–B. Turn the calibrated

Fig 9 How the compass shows the line of route to follow

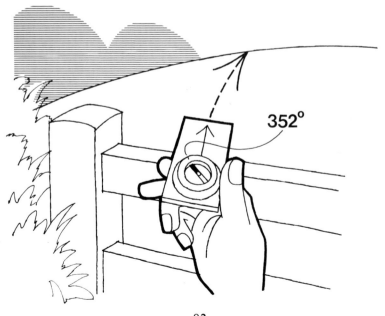

352°

dial so that the red lines beneath the compass needle are parallel with the grid lines on the map. This operation corresponds to that section of the earlier exercise where we were establishing the angle relative to grid north of our desired direction of travel. The direction arrow on the Silva compass now shows us the angle to follow on the ground, and we have so far used the compass simply as a protractor.

The next steps make use of the Silva compass as a magnetic direction finder. Lift it from the map and turn the whole instrument round until the magnetic needle points to 352° (this takes care of the difference between magnetic north and grid north). The direction arrow now shows the line of our route (Fig 9) and we can begin to follow it, checking frequently to see that the needle still points to 352° and that the line of the direction arrow is being followed. In theory B should be reached without further reference to the map. In practice, however, it is a good idea to keep the map orientated so that as features come into view— such as the woods on the far side of the hill, which would appear as the ridge is crossed—they can be used to verify your position and direction. Remember the rule—keep aware of your position on the map as accurately as you can establish it. As far as possible, use the map for navigation and the compass as an adjunct when it becomes necessary.

Other Uses of a Compass

Once the use of the Silva compass for basic direction finding has been mastered, the other uses it can be put to become quite straightforward. Orientating the map is one example. So far this process has been described in terms of visual alignment of the map with identifiable features in the landscape. With a Silva compass, a quicker and more obvious method is to place the centre of the dial over your position on the map so that the red lines below the dial are parallel with the grid lines of the map. Turn map and compass together until the red needle points to 352°. The map is now orientated.

From time to time you may want to check a feature that you can see in the distance with what is shown on the map. For example, the map may show two churches with spires, only one of which is visible from a point on the route being followed. The Silva compass can be used to find out which of the two churches you are looking at. First, hold the compass so that its direction arrow points towards the church spire. Without shifting the direction arrow from its target, turn the dial so that the red compass needle points to 352°. Then, without worrying any more about the compass needle, place the compass on the map so that the centre of the dial is over your position and the red lines are parallel with the grid lines. The direction arrow will then lie over or point to the map symbol representing the church that is visible to you.

It is worth practising with exercises of this kind to get to appreciate the twofold function of the Silva compass. The first steps in the above procedure use the compass as a magnetic direction finder to establish the bearing of a feature that can be seen in the distance. When the dial is turned to point the needle to 352°, the reading on the dial in line with the direction arrow gives the compass bearing for the feature.

The next steps use the Silva compass as a protractor. By laying it over the map in the way described you are in effect measuring off an angle from your position on the map. You may have noticed that this two-stage procedure—magnetic direction finder first, then protractor—is exactly the reverse of the technique used earlier for finding a direction over the hillside from the map. Then you used the instrument first as a protractor on the map to establish the angle of bearing across the hill, and next as a magnetic direction finder to show the right direction to follow on the ground.

Another example of the use of this technique—checking the direction of features in the landscape with the map—is in finding out whether you are following the right path through, for example, woodland or heathland. Point the direction arrow of the Silva compass along the direction of the path ahead, take the bearing by turning the dial until the needle reads 352°, and then lay the compass over the map with red lines parallel with grid lines (a routine you will be getting used to by now). If the direction arrow falls along the line of the path as marked on the map, you are almost certainly on the right path. If the angle does not tally, you are not where you thought you were on the map, and are probably following the wrong path. Your urgent need then is to ascertain your correct position, and there are several ways of doing this.

Finding Your Position with a Compass

Suppose that you have broken the golden rule in map and compass navigation and lost track of your position on the map. The Silva compass can often help to establish your position, the exact method used depending on your circumstances.

If you are travelling along a linear feature such as a clear path or ridge, and you want to establish your position on it, take a bearing on a conspicuous landmark—a church tower or prominent hilltop perhaps—by pointing the direction arrow of the compass at it and turning the dial until the needle points to 352°. Then lay the compass on the map with red lines parallel with the grid lines and with one edge of the compass passing through the symbol for the chosen landmark. The point where this edge of the compass intersects the linear feature you are on gives you your position on the map.

If you are not following such a distinct linear feature, locating your position on the map becomes that much more difficult. Suppose that there are at least two identifiable landmarks in the surrounding landscape. Take a bearing on one of these with the Silva compass and place the compass on the map as described in the last paragraph. Draw a pencil line on the map along the edge of the compass that passes through the landmark symbol. You are somewhere along that line. Repeat this procedure for the other identifiable landmark. The point at which the two pencil lines cross on the map should give your position. As a check it is worth repeating the exercise again with a third feature if you can spot one. In theory the three lines should then intersect at one point, but in practice a small triangle will be formed by the three lines. Take the centre of this triangle as your position.

The worst moments to lose track of your position are when

crossing wild open country with no features you can identify on the map, or when mist blankets out any features there may be. Unfortunately there is no sure way of locating your position on the map in these circumstances. The compass will enable you to orientate the map, and will tell you the direction you are travelling in. If your route has been a fairly direct one, you can take a guess at your position by estimating the distance you have travelled in this known direction from your last known position. Estimate the distance by the time that has elapsed since you set out from this position.

The form of the land around, and the steepness of the slope you are on, can also offer clues, if you can match them with contour patterns on the map. Together map and compass should normally enable you to work out a comparatively safe and quick way to a metalled road or to lower and clearer ground. If you are lost on a mountain in bad weather conditions, the best advice is usually to take shelter and sit it out, but throughout lowland Britain and over much of the uplands careful use of map and compass will nearly always see you back to safety quite soon.

7 What to Wear and What to Take

In deciding what to wear for country walking, your outward appearance counts for nothing. The first essential is that you should feel comfortable, to enjoy the walk and end the day without aches and blisters. The second is that clothing and footwear should keep you safe and well protected from the elements, considerations that will vary enormously according to where you are walking.

It is a fact that for a short walk in easy lowland country no very special gear is needed at all. You go in serviceable clothes, knowing that you might meet mud or brambles. You take a plastic mac in case it rains when you are far from shelter, and stout shoes or wellingtons that you know will be comfortable for a few miles. Thus, without any conscious 'dressing up', your needs are quite adequately met. Indeed, if you are walking muddy paths, wellingtons will serve you better than the most expensive of leather walking boots.

Lowland Walking

Although for lowland walking hardly any items could be called essential, there are some that commend themselves for convenience. Take basic clothing first. For all-purpose wear, trousers of a wool or tweed material are best, though other materials will do, provided they retain their warmth when wet. Jeans are definitely out on this score; when wet they cling and soon leave you feeling very cold about the legs. Most female ramblers find slacks preferable to skirts. If you do opt for a skirt, make sure that it is cut wide enough to cope with some clambering over awkward stiles or gates.

For summer wear, shorts can be more comfortable than long trousers, and even have some advantages if you have occasion to walk through growing crops heavy with rain or dew that can quickly saturate other wear. You will soon realise the disadvant-

Youngsters like to dress up properly for a ramble – like these
two well-shod children on a West Riding 'Kiddiwalk'

ages in wearing shorts, however, when you find your path over-grown with nettles or brambles. Then, alas, even a stout stick will not protect your limbs from stings and scratches, and you will envy the people with legs well covered. So your clothing really depends on the nature of the paths you expect to walk along.

Temperature is another factor to allow for. Even if the day does not warm up, the chances are that you will, and the woolly you started on a summer ramble with will soon come off. In winter you need to provide for more variation in temperature, and you will certainly be wearing or carrying a woollen jumper. In fact two thin sweaters are preferable to one thick one, as this allows you to take off one or both, according to how the day develops. For further warmth, woollen gloves or mittens and a woollen pom-pom hat or beret will take care of your extremities. Be sure to take them.

A good showerproof walking jacket or anorak will make a sensible buy as soon as you start rambling regularly. With a hood for wind and rain protection, it avoids the need to get out the plastic mac every time a shower starts, and the sensible pockets will be handy for holding maps and guides, gloves, camera accessories and all the other small items you like to keep by you.

With woollies coming on and off, a waterproof or two, a book of wild flowers and perhaps some sandwiches for lunch, most walkers will need a simple means of carrying things around. A grip or shoulder bag will do, but a small rucksack makes more sense. It leaves both arms free (people like to swing their arms when walking) and you can soon forget you are carrying anything at all when the load is on your shoulders.

Hill Walking

In the hills suitable clothing becomes critically important, and the factor of safety must be considered along with comfort. Hill walking will bring greater extremes of weather and temperature than lowland walking; even in summer the mountain tops can be very cold places. On the other hand, an energetic climb up a long slope will make you very warm, so good mountain wear must allow changes in ventilation, for comfort. The first essential in protective clothing is to keep the high winds out, so that the layers you wear underneath can retain their 'blanket' of warm air and your body heat is not drawn away. Cheap plastic outer wear will do this, but has the big disadvantage of causing condensation to form inside, so that it is never pleasant to wear for any period. Windproof jackets and anoraks in one of the specially treated cotton fabrics such as 'Ventile' will protect while allowing you to 'breathe' through the material, so that for most purposes they make the best choice. The material is in fact the main reason for the wide variations in prices, and it pays to buy an anorak with the right properties.

Boots are also considered essential for hill walking. They give extra support to the ankles, which meet unaccustomed strains when rough ground turns them to many different angles. The beginner ending a day in the hills with aching ankles will know one good reason why boots are recommended there. The tough going would also disintegrate ordinary footwear in no time, and, most important, the walk may well be over wet rock surfaces where smooth-soled shoes would slip treacherously. A sprained ankle could then easily result. So well designed walking boots with the generally approved kind of moulded composition soles will be your number one investment for hill walking.

Now to look more closely at some of the specialised walking wear.

Boots

Good leather walking boots are not cheap—today you must expect to pay upwards of £20 for them—but they will last much longer and withstand more punishment than shoes, so you will get your money's worth. Once broken in, you will find them just as comfortable, too.

Whichever boots you choose, they should have moulded rubber soles at least $\frac{1}{2}$in thick, with a deep 'tread' pattern and a low heel. Soles of the 'Vibram' or 'Commando' type will give you at least 1,000 miles of wear before needing to be replaced. Uppers should be of thick but supple leather that can be greased, and there should be sponge rubber or felt padding round the ankles. The tongues should be of light supple leather, sewn in right up to the top so that water cannot seep in around them, and the boots should be leather-lined throughout. These are the essentials to look for.

Boots should always be worn with two pairs of socks, a thinner one next your feet and a thicker woollen one over that. When buying boots, therefore, it is important that you try them on with socks of at least 3-ply thickness pulled on over a normal thin pair. Walking gear shops will know this, and have some thick oversocks ready for your use. Otherwise take a pair of your own. You will find that you will need boots a half or whole size larger than you normally take. There should be ample room to move your toes inside them without their feeling loose, and there should be a good space between the toes and the inside of the toecaps. See that the new boots fit closely round the instep when laced, and that the sides do not meet over the tongue, so that there is room left for adjustment.

If you are buying boots for growing youngsters, it is a good idea to start them off with a pair that fits comfortably over three pairs of socks. Then, by leaving one pair off as their feet grow, the boots can last them a year or two longer.

If you are wise, you will break in new boots on a number of short walks before wearing them on a holiday or on longer walks. Some 30 miles need to be covered in gentle stages before leather boots are shaped to your feet and begin to feel really comfortable. If you feel a blister coming on while breaking in your boots, attend to it right away by applying an adhesive plaster or foam plastic.

It is usually at the ankles that new boots cause the most discomfort, and at first it can be worth while lacing them in a special fashion, as follows: lace them up firmly for the first few hooks or eyelets, to about the usual height of a laced shoe; then make a reef knot and just tie the top of the bootlace slackly but sufficiently to give a little ankle support. Within a few days of wearing the ankle bone will have made a depression in the leg of the boot, and you can then lace them firmly all the way up.

If you have no time to break your boots in by walking, you can hurry the process up by making them more immediately flexible in the following way. Fill a deep bowl with sufficient tepid water to cover the boots, then put them on, lacing them tightly over a pair of thick walking socks; pull up a chair, sit down and soak your booted feet in the water for half an hour. By this time the soaked and softened leather will have formed itself to the shape of your feet. Lift the boots out of the water, unlace them as fully as you can and take them off, trying to avoid spoiling the moulded shape. Wipe off surplus water and leave the boots on their sides to dry. Before they are fully dry, apply dubbin or a wax polish, rubbing well in but not so as to affect the shape you have moulded them into. Then leave them to dry fully.

For long life, treat your boots regularly with a waterproofing dubbin and/or a leather oil or goose fat, to keep them supple. None of the proprietory brands of waterproof dressing render boots entirely impervious to water; even when heavily treated it is only a matter of time before they become thoroughly sodden in really wet conditions. Even so, regular application of dubbin does help to preserve the leather. Take care, though, only to treat the leather, as some dubbins have been known to rot the stitching.

All dressings are best applied when the leather is in a damp but otherwise clean condition. It is strongly recommended that dressings be applied with the fingers or hand, and well rubbed in, rather than by brush or rag. The warmth of the hand helps to drive the dressing into the pores of the leather. Whatever dressing you use, it should be applied inside as well as out, and particular attention should be paid to the undersides of the tongues and the upper rim of the heels, where blisters are most likely to be caused if the leather is not kept supple.

As soon as you return from a ramble, wash the mud off your boots with cold or lukewarm water, mop off the surplus and apply dressing before the boots dry. Never put your boots away bone-dry and caked with mud, especially if you have been walking in boggy country; bogs contain acid that causes considerable damage to both the leather and the stitching. Never use heat, even from a radiator, to hurry the drying-out process. If your boots are still damp when you need them next, leave it to foot pressure and your own body heat to finish the drying.

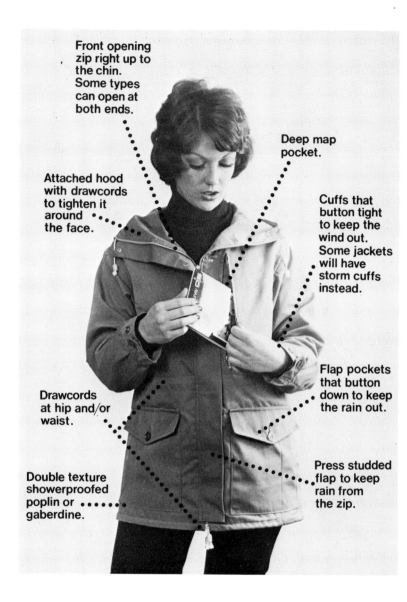

Front opening zip right up to the chin. Some types can open at both ends.

Deep map pocket.

Attached hood with drawcords to tighten it around the face.

Cuffs that button tight to keep the wind out. Some jackets will have storm cuffs instead.

Drawcords at hip and/or waist.

Flap pockets that button down to keep the rain out.

Double texture showerproofed poplin or gaberdine.

Press studded flap to keep rain from the zip.

Features of a good rambling anorak

When they are not in use for a time, pack your boots tightly with old newspaper, so as to keep them moulded to their original shape.

Breeches

Knee-length breeches are more comfortable and practical than long trousers for rambling, and particularly for fell walking. Most breeches fasten just below the knee with elasticated adhesive adjusters or buckles, and long socks, elasticated at knee height, complete the outfit. Materials used for breeches include worsted, whipcord, needlecord and moleskin, but the last-named, although heavy and hard-wearing, is probably more appropriate for rock climbing than rambling. Most breeches are suitable for all-the-year wear, but if you can afford two pairs, it makes sense to choose lightweight cloth for summer wear and heavier material for winter.

Overtrousers

Whether you elect to wear breeches or long trousers, nylon over-trousers will be useful in keeping them dry in wet weather, with the added merit of being windproof, thus keeping your legs warm even when the wind blows cold. Overtrousers should be elasticated at the waist and zipped at the bottom of the legs so that you can put them on without removing your boots. As they weigh only a few ounces and take very little room, you have nothing to lose by carrying a pair with you wherever you ramble.

Gaiters

Rather different from the model worn by bishops, the ramblers' gaiter, sometimes called a stop-tout, is made of canvas or nylon. It reaches down from the knee to cover part of the boot, and is particularly useful in preventing water, stones, mud and vegetation from creeping into your boots or getting on to your socks.

Anoraks

So widely fashionable today, they can hardly be regarded as specialised wear only for ramblers. For hill walking, choose one in a good showerproof material, with a hood provided with a

Sensible outer wear for bad weather in the hills. Rainproof 'Hill-Helly' smock with hood and matching breeches, all in orange PVC cloth. (A cagoule is a similar but longer garment, dropping to knee length. Overtrousers which reach to the ankles are also very useful in wet conditions)

drawcord to close it snugly around your face when necessary. Cuffs should be tight-fitting, provided with tightening adjustment or inner elasticated cuffs to keep wind out. Pockets should be plentiful, with rain-protecting flaps and at least one of a size to take an OS map in a readily accessible position. Most walkers prefer the type that can be opened down the front, as this provides welcome ventilation when it gets warmer. Prices will vary greatly according to the material and its proofing.

Cagoules

The cagoule is a knee-length smock with a hood, usually in waterproof nylon or polyurethane. Worn over an anorak in heavy rain, it is preferable to a cape, but, being completely impervious to moisture, it should only be put on in very wet or windy weather, otherwise condensation inside it will become a discomfort. A cagoule also has safety aspects when taken on a hill walk. Its bright colour makes it easier for you to be seen, easier for companions to follow you in mist, for example. And if you need to stop in really foul weather, you can tuck your feet up inside it and be completely protected from the elements.

Rucksacks

For a day's walking, or any expedition when you need carry only a light load, a small frameless rucksack with a capacity of about 20 litres will be ideal. Most types will have one or two outside pockets for the small items you want to keep readily available, and the material will generally be cotton or nylon. Nylon has the advantage that it is virtually waterproof when new, but it is not as hard-wearing as cotton. The frameless type is not suitable for heavy loads because it lies directly on your back, where it can chafe and cause perspiration. But packed carefully to ensure that no hard or sharp-edged objects are sticking into you, it will carry a light load for many miles, comfortably.

The larger rucksacks are provided with a frame in aluminium or steel—sometimes an integral part of the rucksack, sometimes a separate piece to which the bag is fastened. The frame carries

97

the load in a better position on your shoulders, and keeps it out of contact with your back, so that air has a space to circulate in. For packing a really heavy load on a walking tour etc, the modern 'high-loader' rucksack may look formidable but its principle is very sound. By widening towards the top it carries much of the load above shoulder level where it is the least strain, enabling the wearer to walk without having to double up. The capacity of a back-packing rucksack of this kind will be around 60 litres. Naturally the framed type is very much more expensive.

Ideally a well balanced rucksack should place the load you carry directly over your centre of gravity. Most rucksacks are adjustable to some extent, but getting the right fit is important, so go to a good specialist retailer who will know how to fit you correctly.

What to Pack

When packing a rucksack, remember the aim of carrying weight as high as possible, and try to keep the lightest items at the lowest level and heavy objects at the top. Do not trust to waterproofing; put clothes and any other items that damp could harm into plastic bags before you pack them. If you are heading for a day in the hills, think of that temperature drop and be sure you have packed at least one more woolly than you think you need. Except on long summer days, a torch makes a sensible addition, too, just in case the walk takes longer than you expect and ends in darkness.

There are a few items that can take a permanent place in one of those outside pockets, especially for hill walking—some extra high-energy food like chocolate, mint cake or glucose tablets, a whistle and a simple first-aid kit ready to deal with blisters or a strained ankle. You never know when you might need them, and, once in the rucksack, they can happily live there permanently.

Just one other item is worth a recommendation, for lowland and hill walking alike. That is the transparent map case, which you can slip an opened map or guidebook into, to protect it from the elements and keep it clean and flat. Even in rain or snow there are occasions when you must get the map out, and a few

Types of rucksack. A and C are typical high-loader frame rucksacks,
B is a separate frame and high capacity sac, D is a smaller
daysac and E is a simple duffle bag, also suitable for a day walk,
slung from the shoulder

minutes of soaking will reduce it to a soggy mess unless it is
protected. If you buy one, be sure that it will take the latest OS
maps opened out for reading. Metric maps are slightly larger
than their predecessors.

Major Rambling Gear Suppliers

It is not always easy to find a dependable supplier in your own
neighbourhood. If you have difficulty, refer to this short list of
centrally placed specialist suppliers, all of whom can be relied
on to stock the lines reviewed in this book, and to give sound
advice on them.

Birmingham   YHA Sales, 35 Cannon Street, Birmingham B2
    5EE.
Bristol Joseph Bryant, The Outdoor Centre, Colston Street,
    Bristol.

Ellis Brigham, 162 Whiteladies Road, Bristol.

Liverpool   Ellis Brigham, 73 Bold Street, Liverpool 1.

London   YHA Sales, 14 Southampton Street, WC2E 7HY.

Pindisports, 14 Holborn, EC1.

Alpine Sports Ltd, 309/311 Brompton Road, SW3.

Manchester   YHA Sales, 36/38 Fountain Street, Manchester M2 2BE.

Ellis Brigham, 6/14 Cathedral Street, Manchester M4 3FU.

North Wales   Joe Brown, Menai Hall, Llanberis, Gwynedd.

Glasgow   Blacks of Greenock, 132 St Vincent Street, Glasgow G2 5HF.

Edinburgh   Graham Tiso, 44 Rodney Street, Edinburgh 7.

8 Taking to the Hills

Relatively few of us will be able to reach the popular upland areas in a day's journey. The High Peak of Derbyshire is the outstanding exception to this, with over 17 million people living within a 50-mile radius, some virtually within walking distance of the open moors, and all able to contemplate an escape into the hills within an hour or so. To the majority, though, hill country must be explored via a long weekend or a holiday period —a planned expedition entailing a choice of places to stay and decisions on how much of the area we aim to explore in one visit. These are factors that distinguish hill walking from other, less ambitious, styles of countrygoing. Another is the element of caution that must be exercised. The very openness of the country, together with its height, can be a source of danger as well as inspiration.

Temperatures on the hills are always lower than down below in a sheltered valley. If bad weather breaks, it can reach extreme conditions with high winds and driving rain combining to lower the temperature further still. Then the lack of shelter can create real problems. Bad weather can 'brew-up' with unexpected suddenness in the hills; even the regional weather forecast is seldom an accurate guide, as it can take little account of the vagaries of hill country, and local advice is usually more reliable. Local folk know the signs to look for. Cloud and mist can usually be seen building up or rising from the valleys, but, as they arrive, the 'blotting out' effect can be just as disturbing, when only moments before you were admiring a sunlit landscape.

All these characteristics of hill country need not deter anyone from setting out, with some sensible precautions. When you have tramped a high path into the hills shrouded in low cloud, to have the cloud suddenly rise and sweep away, revealing all the hidden panorama around you for the first time, you will know an elation, a lifting of the spirit that perhaps only the hills in their wayward way can provide. Hills without their attendant weather would have little joy to offer the hill walker. So do not be put off but go prepared, with the proper equipment, and, if you are a newcomer to the hills, try to underestimate rather than over-estimate your capabilities. Be prepared to turn back if the weather is clearly taking a turn for the worse.

Winter lingers longer in the hills, and, as well as being a time when views of exceptional clarity and beauty can be gained, is also a time for ice and snow and the associated hazards. Exposed and steep hill walks that are safe enough in summer will be suitable in winter only for experienced fell walkers armed with ice axes and crampons, and well versed in their use. So follow only the easiest of routes until you too have begun to gain their experience, and above all be guided by Chapter 7 in deciding what to wear and what to take with you.

To plan a day in the hills you need a good clear map and some emerging skill in interpreting it, particularly in understanding what the contours are trying to tell you. You do not, for example, want to find yourself descending into a valley, only to climb an unnecessary 1,000ft up out of it again, when you could more easily and enjoyably have followed the level contours round the head of the valley. Climbing and descending in hills is always harder work than walking on the level, even when this means walking a bit further in terms of distance on the map.

Allow yourself plenty of time. It is better to have an hour or two left to saunter back at the end of the day than to rush the last stage of a walk, when you are feeling the most tired, to get back before darkness falls or a mealtime arrives. An idea of the length of time needed for the walk can be gained by using the simple formula by which 1 hour is allowed for every 3 miles covered on the map, and a further half hour added for every 1,000ft of ascent. Thus a walk that appears to be 9 miles long from the map, and to include a total of 3,000ft of climbing, should take around $4\frac{1}{2}$ hours. You may find from your own experience that this rule is too generous, or that the allowance is not enough. The principle is never to forget to allow the extra time needed for climbing and descending, particularly over rough ground.

If, despite taking all sensible precautions, you do find yourself in difficulty, you should be aware of the standard mountain distress signal, which consists of six blasts on a whistle, repeated every minute. The reply is three blasts. Another word of advice if you are setting out for the hills is to leave a note with someone to indicate where you intend to finish up and the route you plan to follow. If you are starting out from your car, leave the note tucked behind the windscreen. If you are staying at a youth hostel, record the information in a log book kept for just this purpose. It makes sense, even if you are quite convinced that nothing is going to happen to you. Many tragedies in hill country could have been largely averted if rescue parties had known early enough that someone was missing, and had had a good idea where to look or where they might be sheltering.

Ways of Exploring

How do you set about exploring our hill country on foot? Firstly, a study of the appropriate maps will show that, although much of the land is open, there are, even so, many footpaths and bridle-ways crossing the hills, suggesting easy walking or at least easy-to-find routes. This is sometimes so, although our OS maps do not follow the policy of some European maps of popular areas in indicating which paths are easily discernible on the ground and which are not. Neither is waymarking as common in this country, although some routes may be defined with cairns to guide you over open stretches.

If you are wondering whether a particular hill path is easy to find and follow, enquire locally. Some routes are well trodden, and even over hard rock the marks left by the passage of thousands of eager boots over the years will guide you. Perhaps it will be one of the old ways up over a mountain pass, like the packhorse way that climbs over Grisedale Hause in the Lake District to link Grasmere and Patterdale beneath the slopes of Helvellyn, or the miners' track that crosses from Llyn Ogwen over to Pen-y-Gwryd via the shoulder of Glyder Fach in Snowdonia. Perhaps it will be a favourite route up into the

overleaf: Ramblers follow the well-trodden track by Styhead Tarn down to Seathwaite in the Lake District

mountains, like the familiar track from Seathwaite at the head of Borrowdale that takes hill-lovers by the thousand up to Sty Head, where the great central Lakeland heights of Gable, Glaramara and the Scafell Pikes enclose you invitingly. It might indeed be a truly ancient way, like the Roman road that climbs over Cam Fell on the Yorkshire Moors to march on down to the camp at Bainbridge, taken in turn by packhorse traders and now by walkers of the Pennine Way.

By following tracks like these you can gain the true feel of the high remote hills, with little concern over losing your way. But still, the path that turns off our well worn track may not be visible on the ground at all. The grassy summit ridge that tempts you with its panoramic views and breezy openness may not be followed by a recognised footpath, even though it can be seen to offer easy going. The best of hill walking is essentially open-country walking like this, so map-reading experience really is important to enjoy it to the full.

As most visitors to hill areas are there for a period of holiday rather than a day visit, an obvious question will be—Should you stay in one centre or move on day by day? There are obvious advantages in staying at one well placed point and exploring the hills around. With a lot of climbing to do, you will be very much aware of the weight you are carrying with you, and touring from a centre means that you need take only essentials. But choose your centre carefully, at a confluence of valleys perhaps, so that several directions open up entirely different walking possibilities. Then a satisfying week could be spent in the hills. From Buttermere village in the Lake District, for example, paths radiate in all directions, by the shores of Crummock Water or Buttermere, over Scarth Gap into Ennerdale or on to Great Gable, round Fleetwith Pike to Honister Pass, up Sail Beck or on to the massive summit of Grasmoor.

Equally there are attractions in moving on, to tour from point to point. One great satisfaction in hill walking is to make the kind of journey that wayfarers have followed through the ages, crossing from one valley over the high passes to another, with a sense of distance covered and obstacles overcome to reach a destination. From Buttermere village the path over Scarth Gap continues around the head of Ennerdale, over the dramatic Black Sail Pass and down to Wasdale Head. It is an exciting walk, typical of many such valley-to-valley walks in the Lake District, a few hours' walking linking spots that would necessitate at least a 30-mile car drive for lesser mortals.

The further alternative of using the car as a start to a hill walk is perfectly practical, and indeed popular today. It provides a variation on the 'centre' theme, because your walk has to be planned as a circular route, returning to wherever the car has been left. Parking, too, is something that must be done with consideration both for fellow visitors and for the farmer in the dale. Narrow valley roads and tracks along which he needs access for a tractor or even a flock of sheep can be completely blocked by thoughtlessly parked cars. Even mountain rescue teams have found their way blocked at critical times, so all in all it must be said that the most welcome visitor to the hills is the one who comes car-less.

Overnight accommodation is seldom hard to find in hill country, at least in the popular areas. Throughout spring and summer these remote communities find welcome extra income from catering for visitors, and many a hill farm or cottage will be happy to provide bed and breakfast (and parking space) at very reasonable terms. One advantage in farmhouse accommodation is that nobody is the least bit concerned if ramblers return with a healthy covering of mud, and appetites to match. Several annual publications offer useful lists of suitable country-style accommodation—cottages, pubs and guest houses etc—including the *Bed and Breakfast Guide* published each spring by the Ramblers' Association, with addresses used and recommended by their members.

The time of year

The hill walker's ideal day will be one with clear distant vision to make the most of the high viewpoints he reaches, and the flowing, constantly changing pattern of sunshine and cloud that gives the most dramatic effect to a landscape of rolling hills. These conditions are most likely in the spring. Later, in high summer, heat haze may obscure the distance, and by tradition the hill country of the north and west will experience its wettest cloudiest weather.

Where the valley scenery is especially fine, then spring will undoubtedly show it at its best, with the fresh greens of grass and foliage, and young lambs in the low meadows. But remember that spring comes late in the northern hills, and on the hills themselves colour will most probably come from the gorse, heather and ever-invading bracken. In early spring the dead bracken will still be adding its warm colouring to the hills, but by June the fresh green fronds will be coming through fast. By late October the bracken will have turned a rich autumnal red and the hills will be at their most colourful. Throughout May and June the yellow flowers and heavy scent of gorse will be prominent features of some uplands, while the heather will add its haze of colour to hillsides from July to September.

The upland areas

A glance at the map will show you that our high lands are mainly grouped to the west, the midlands and the north. They derive their location, and their individual character, from the geology that raised them from the surrounding lowlands. Thus the two great moorland areas of the West Country—Exmoor and Dartmoor—offer very different landscapes. The sandstone of Exmoor produces gently rolling heather-clad hills and well wooded combes, while the bleak barren plateau of Dartmoor is a characteristic granite landscape, a fact underlined by the tumbled outcrops that crown each tor, where the bedrock granite stands exposed.

Across the Bristol Channel Wales offers an even greater degree of contrast, between the grass-covered heights of the Brecon Beacons, which seem literally to have been carved from the Old Red Sandstone, and the rugged expanses of exposed volcanic rock that form the ranges of Snowdonia in the north. The term 'highland' covers an extreme variety of walking country, from the gently invigorating to the strenuously exciting.

The softly contoured lines that characterise the limestone hills can be followed in a pattern extending from Somerset across central England into Yorkshire. Whether forming the Mendips, pierced by steep gorges and underground streams that have formed the great cave systems, or the high centre of the North Yorkshire Moors, the scenery clearly has a 'family likeness'. Other highland areas offer their own geological contrasts. The Derbyshire Peak District, for example, begins with grey limestone in the south, providing the white walls and cliffs of the 'White Peak'; then, further north, the gritstone edges begin to appear over sandstone; and finally come the great peat-covered plateaux of Millstone Grit that form Kinder and Bleaklow. Thus, within the compass of a few miles, the walker in Peakland can choose between paths that follow the lush river valleys of Dove or Manifold, deep cut into the limestone, those following the high rolling sandstone ridges above Castleton, or a really tough route into the wilderness of the old grouse moors.

Further north still, only a few miles separate the great dome of the Lake District—slate and other hard rocks worn and glacially scoured into broad deep-sided valleys—from the contrasting scenery of the Yorkshire Dales. Here the softer limestone, shale and sandstone hills are capped in places by Millstone Grit that forms the sudden upflinging of heights such as Penyghent and Ingleborough.

Any description of our hill country is akin to a description of the National Parks. The ten Parks of England and Wales embrace most of our finest upland scenery, and as a visitor you will find services to help you, including car parks, picnic sites and information centres that give advice on accommodation etc. The legislation that provided the National Parks does not cover Scotland, but of course much superbly wild mountain walking can be found north of the border—the great granite plateau of the Cairngorms, Ben Nevis soaring sheer above its beautiful glen, the peaks and lochs of the Central Highlands with Glen Coe the most darkly moving of all the passes, or for easier walking, the pretty lake scenery of the Trossachs or the gentle Pentland Hills.

Now, as a brief review of the hill areas, we start in the north-west and travel clockwise around the country.

The Lake District

Britain's largest National Park is also considered by many ramblers to contain our finest mountain walking. Within a very compact group there are no less than seventy-four peaks over 2,000ft, among them the only 3,000ft mountains in England. From the central dome of old rock containing the highest peaks, deep glacial valleys radiate out like the spokes of a vast wheel, and in them glitter the long lakes that give the district its familiar name. The variety of hard rocks, slates and volcanics, gives each mountain an individual character which enthusiasts will instantly recognise. The broad valleys are lovely in themselves with their old stone farmsteads, a few still with their spinning galleries.

Over 90,000 acres within the Park are owned or protected by the National Trust, some measure of the high value placed on these landscapes. The YHA has a network of twenty-two hostels, ranging from the handsome new purpose-built Patterdale Hostel to tiny remote Black Sail Hut in the shadow of Pillar, allowing great scope for walking tours. The hills and sheep grazings are almost entirely open, and the obvious mountain paths and ridge routes are all well walked; indeed a few of the most used access tracks suffer from erosion problems. There is ample scope for valley walking, the paths up Langdale, the Watendlath valley or upper Borrowdale being good examples; and equal scope for following the banks of several of the lakes—Buttermere, Crummock Water, Ullswater and Ennerdale Water, for instance. The well known passes offer relatively easy mountain expeditions: examples are the long walk over Stake Pass from Langdale to Borrowdale, or the Black Sail and Scarth Gap Passes from Buttermere over to Wastwater. For sheer exhilaration try the ridge walks—over High Street, the very exposed Crinkle Crags, or down from Helvellyn via famous Striding Edge. Something for every taste—a true walkers' paradise!

Since Wordsworth's day the fells have been the subject of many guidebooks, but none more detailed than those of Mr A. Wainwright, who divided the area into seven sections, as described below.

Northern. Two major peaks, Skiddaw (3,053ft) and

Blencathra (2,847ft) dominate an area untypical of Lakeland scenery and having more in common with Pennine moorlands. The northern fells are little frequented and a good place to avoid crowds on a busy summer weekend. The centres to base yourself at are Bassenthwaite, Caldbeck and Threlkeld, small and pleasant Cumbrian villages, or Keswick, a fair-sized town with useful 'outdoor' shops and good transport, which makes it convenient as a touring centre for Borrowdale and most of the Lakes.

Far Eastern. The dominant feature of this group is the High Street ridge, straight enough for the Romans to have used as their road between Ambleside and Penrith, though what the legionaires thought of marching at 2,700ft is not recorded. Today it is a long but easy grass track. The ground slopes away to the east down to the A6 and M6, while to the west of the main ridge a series of spurs leads down to the Kirkstone Pass road, which at 1,489ft is the highest road pass in the Lake District. Touring centres are Patterdale, with its hotels and hostels; Hartsop, where the best known path climbs to High Street; and also Bampton, Staveley, Windermere and Ambleside.

Eastern. Another group basically composed of one long ridge with offshoots, but this time the ridge is the highest and longest in the District, running from Threlkeld south over Helvellyn (3,118ft) and Fairfield (2,863ft) among other fells before descending to the Rothay valley near Ambleside. The western side of the ridge north of Grisedale Tarn, where the pass is used by an old packhorse trail from Grasmere to Patterdale, is steep and relatively uninteresting, with afforestation above Thirlmere, a reservoir for Manchester since the end of the nineteenth century. But the eastern side is much more dramatic, with a series of coves divided by narrow ridges, of which Striding Edge has acquired a special claim to fame. South of Grisedale Tarn two ridges lead from Fairfield to the Rothay, the complete and popular traverse of the ridges being known as the Fairfield Horseshoe. The centres are Ambleside; Grasmere, with its two youth hostels; Stanah, where the old Sticks Pass track climbs over the ridge to Glenridding; Threlkeld; and Patterdale, near where the superbly situated Helvellyn Hostel stands among the old Greenside mine workings, with tracks direct to the summit ridge.

111

Southern. This group consists of the range of mountains surrounding Eskdale and containing the highest and most rugged hills in the Lake District, and also the group of fells between Coniston Water and the Duddon Valley known as the Coniston Fells. The Eskdale Fells surround upper Eskdale, where the valley turns north beyond Hardknott Pass. The major fells are Scafell (3,162ft), Scafell Pike (at 3,210ft the highest place in England), Great End (2,984ft), Esk Pike (2,903ft), Bowfell (2,960ft) and Crinkle Crags (2,816ft). These are true mountains, with the going everywhere rocky and difficult, and the time needed for walks correspondingly longer.

The Coniston Fells, on the other hand, present a smoother outline, with a number of ridges meeting at Swirl How. The walking over these ridges is grassy and easy in the main to the highest peak in the group, Coniston Old Man (2,635ft). Coniston village is the obvious centre for exploring this area, and again a youth hostel is situated remotely up the Coppermines Valley beneath the Old Man. Boot in Eskdale is, surprisingly, the terminus of a narrow gauge rail link down to Ravenglass on the coast, a delightful way to reach a mountain centre. A well used track leads from Boot over to Wasdale Head, another popular centre for the area. Indeed the centres for exploring the high Eskdale fells lie each at the beginning of one of the tracks up to Sty Head and Angle Tarn: Wasdale with its track by Lingmell Beck, then Borrowdale with its approach via gloomy Styhead Tarn, and Langdale with its stony scramble up Rossett Gill.

Western. The fells on either side of Ennerdale, together with the offshoots from the main ridge, form this group. Ennerdale itself is dark with the gloom of conifers planted 40 years ago, and its north side is uniformly steep and relatively dull. But the further side of the same fells is as interesting as the southern side of Ennerdale, with crags and coves in abundance. The best known mountains are Great Gable (2,949ft), Pillar (2,927ft), Steeple (2,687ft), High Stile (2,644ft) and the two Red Pikes, one overlooking Buttermere and the other Wasdale. From the head of Scarth Gap Pass a fine but rugged ridge walk leads up to High Stile, while for the less adventurous pleasant paths lead above Haystacks to Innominate Tarn, a delightful spot with views over

112

the head of Ennerdale to Great Gable. The best centres are Buttermere; Hassness by the lakeshore, a guest house run by the Ramblers' Association especially for walking holidays; Gatesgarth Farm, at the foot of Honister Pass; or the Youth Hostel up on Honister Hause. Ennerdale Bridge is rather far from the fells, but there are youth hostels better situated in the valley, at Gillerthwaite and Black Sail. Borrowdale and Wasdale Head are also possible centres.

North-western. This group is noted for the excellence of its ridge walks and straight-sided fells. Surrounded by the lakes of Bassenthwaite, Derwentwater, Buttermere, Crummock Water and Loweswater, the principal fells are Grasmoor (2,791ft), Grisedale Pike (2,593ft) and Dale Head (2,473ft). This area can be explored from several points: from Keswick, Braithwaite or several addresses that offer accommodation in the Newlands Valley; or from Buttermere, Loweswater, Lorton or even Cockermouth, although the last-named is rather far from the fells.

Central. The core of the Lake District, bound by Borrowdale, Thirlmere and Langdale, does not contain any especially high fells, although in the twin peaks of Langdale Pikes it has probably the best known of all the Lakeland skylines. From centres in Borrowdale, Langdale or Grasmere, it offers a range of easy hill walks, up to the delightful Watendlath hamlet and on via Blea Tarn; up Easedale Gill; along the ridges above Langdale; up Dungeon Ghyll to Stickle Tarn; and many other variations.

Cheviots

As the northernmost section of the Northumberland National Park, the Cheviot Hills are part of the traditional 'border country' between England and Scotland. The high granite dome that forms the Cheviot itself (2,674ft) has bare moorland falling away around it, cut by the beautiful winding steep-sided valleys of the five burns that rise and radiate out from Cheviot. By Harthope Burn, Breamish or the College valley minor roads provide a starting point for walks into the heart of the Cheviots, for although the walking is easy enough, mainly over grass, this is very remote country with great uninhabited distances to span. The Pennine

Way passes through the area, following the old boundary fence for a while, with a branch visiting the Cheviot itself, before descending into Scotland to end at Kirk Yetholm. This is one of the centres for exploring Cheviot country, with a youth hostel and other accommodation. The little market town of Wooler, also with a hostel, is another popular centre. Other centres are Alnham, Rothbury and Alwinton, with youth hostels at Byrness and Bellingham serving walkers on the Pennine Way and explorers of the hill country around.

North Pennines

Between the Stainmore Gap and the Tyne valley rise the North Pennine hills, a wide, wild and lonely expanse of moorland rising to the highest point on the Pennine Way on the wide featureless plateau of Cross Fell (2,930ft). Walkers will find the main interest in the paths that follow the beautiful river valleys, particularly in upper Teesdale, which has two well known waterfalls—massive High Force with its 70ft drop into a rocky gorge, and Cauldron Snout, a long tumbling cascade. High Cup is a dramatic feature on the escarpment high above the Eden valley and Appleby. Main centres are Barnard Castle, Middleton in Teesdale, Alston and Stanhope. There are youth hostels at Barnard Castle, Alston, Dufton (below High Cup), and Langdon Beck (near High Force).

North York Moors

High moorland occupying a large area to the south of the Teesside conurbation was designated the North York Moors National Park in 1952. The central area is a vast expanse of heather-clad moor, best seen in September for its colour, with broad open valleys, of which Rosedale and Farndale are the best known. Visit upper Farndale for its wild daffodils in Spring. Many 'trods' and ancient ways cross the moor, even an exposed length of Roman road on Wheeldale Moor, and hardy walkers challenge themselves each year with the 40 mile Lyke Wake Walk. For a unique high level walk that follows an even contour mile after mile, follow the bed of the old ironstone railway from Rosedale to Greenhow Bank. But for the most popular walks, follow the steep escarpments, the Cleveland Hills facing north and the Hambledon Hills facing south-west to the Vale of York. There are spectacular views, even though no points reach as high as 1,500ft. The moors are within easy reach of such major centres as Whitby, Scarborough, Pickering, Stokesley or Helmsley, or from valley villages such as Rosedale Abbey, Goathland and Hutton-le-Hole. There are youth hostels at Westerdale on the upper Esk, Whitby, Scarborough, Helmsley, and Wheeldale Lodge, remote in its moorland vale above Goathland.

Yorkshire Dales

680 square miles of the Yorkshire Dales have been a National Park since 1954. In the south fine limestone moorland has distinctive landmarks in the form of the great Millstone Grit hills— Ingleborough (2,373ft), Penyghent (2,273ft) and Whernside (2,419ft). The Craven Fault, a landslip running across the southern Park, creates spectacular scenery in Malham Cove and nearby Goredale Scar. Limestone pavements above the Cove, caves, potholes and underground streams all make for interesting exploring hereabouts. Base yourself on Malham, but avoid the crowds of high summer. The moors are open and easy to walk in the south, peaty and more remote in the north. The old drove ways make for easy high walking from vale to vale; take Mastiles Lane from Malham over to Kilnsey; or tracks from Hawes south to Ribblesdale, or Bainbridge to Wharfedale. The broad dales also make fine footpath walking, especially upper Wharfedale around Buckden; Wensleydale, with its fine falls at Aysgarth and Hardraw near Hawes; and upper Swaledale, with a string of falls near Keld. The major centres are Settle, Malham, Ingleton, Grassington, Kirkby Stephen, Hawes and Askrigg, although many of the dales villages offer simple accommodation. There are hostels at Malham and Stainforth in the south; Linton and Kettlewell in Wharfedale; Hawes, Aysgarth and remote Garsdale Head in Wensleydale; and Keld and Grinton in Swaledale.

overleaf: The distinctive landmark of Penyghent rises from the limestone moorland of the Yorkshire Dales National Park

Peak District

At the southern end of the Pennine chain a broad moorland dome, the Dark Peak, now forms part of the first National Park, set up in 1951. There are no 'peaks' in the Peak District, the great heights of Kinder (2,080ft), Bleaklow (2,060ft) and Black Hill (1,908ft) being flat areas of deep peat groughs, difficult to cross and easy to get lost in. Sandwiched between the conurbations of Manchester and Sheffield, the Dark Peak has long been popular with ramblers, and agreements negotiated by the Park authority now give access to 74 square miles of these moorland tops, once jealously guarded by gamekeepers. Today access is only restricted during the grouse-shooting season; wardens and notices at the access points will tell you which areas are closed on which days. The most rewarding walks on Kinder follow the escarpment, particularly to the north, where views are impressive over the Snake Pass, and weird stone 'tors' are features of the edge. Avoid the deep groughs of the centre unless you like punishment. The Pennine Way starts up from Edale—easy meadow walking at first, but then a steep rough pull up Grindsbrook. The signposted 'bad weather route' makes easier walking via Jacob's Ladder to Kinder Downfall, a popular outing to this exposed waterfall. As well as the gritstone highlands, the gentler sandstone hills above Castleton—Lose Hill, Mam Tor etc—make a good ridge walk, while the characteristic gritstone edges, Stanage Edge in particular, are worth exploring. The best centres are Edale, Glossop, Hayfield and Castleton, with youth hostels at Castleton, Nether Booth in Edale, Crowden in Longdendale, and Langsett; Hagg Farm on the Snake Road is an unusual 'mountain hostel' managed by the Peak Park Board and open to everyone.

Dartmoor

The great granite massif of Dartmoor, over 200 square miles of it, is the only really extensive wilderness area remaining in the south-west. The high moorland is punctuated with granite tors, often eroded into fantastic forms. The highest and remotest section of the moor, in the north-west, has two summits over

2,000ft—High Willhays (2,038ft) and Yes Tor (2,030ft). Walkers will still regard Cranmore Pool as the elusive objective to search for in the very heart of the moor, but this central area is rough peaty going, featureless and often boggy. Weather, too, is to be watched warily. Mist, low cloud and rain can descend with little warning, and it is no coincidence that most of the Devon rivers rise here. Artillery alas, is another hazard! An Army firing range still uses the area from Okehampton south to Great Mis Tor on many days, even in holiday periods. Check notices in local post offices, watch for red flags flying and beware of suspicious metal objects. Antiquities add to the interest of Dartmoor walking. Visit Grimspound, the Bronze Age enclosure a 3-mile tramp over Hameldown from Widecombe. Find the Scorhill stone circle on Gidleigh Common, or the strange double circle of 'grey wethers' below Sittaford Tor. Most Dartmoor walking is rough, over open moor; for easier expeditions, it is best to find the old tracks—the Lich Way that climbs on to the moor from Peter Tavy, the Sandy Way leading up from Holne village and Abbots Way across the southern moor, and others. The centres around the moor are Okehampton, Chagford, Moretonhampstead, Bovey Tracey, Ashburton, Ivybridge and Tavistock, with a little accommodation in moorland villages such as Widecombe. There are youth hostels at Gidleigh, Steps Bridge down in the Teign valley, Tavistock, and Bellever near Postbridge, well up on the moor.

Exmoor

Smallest of our English National Parks, Exmoor is shared between Devon and Somerset, and includes the coastline from Minehead to Combe Martin. The high plateau of sandstone moor, mostly around the 1,300ft height, is open grazing in its central areas, and grassy, heather-clad and relatively easy to walk, rising to its summit at Dunkery Beacon (1,705ft). Enclosed farmland has crept up from the valleys and often has to be crossed before reaching the freedom of the open moor. Deep wooded combes pierce the uplands, sheltering the famous herds of red deer, with streams often swollen by the heavy Exmoor rainfall plunging down steep and pretty ravines to reach the Bristol Channel.

Horner Water and Badgworthy Water in particular offer delightful walking routes up to the high moor, the latter being followed each year by many in search of the Doones of R. D. Blackmore's romance. The folded Exmoor hills make superb cliff scenery as they reach the sea, most of which can only be enjoyed via the waymarked coast path. Exmoor can easily be explored from the coast resorts nestling beneath it—Minehead, Porlock, Lynton or Combe Martin—or from inland centres such as Dulverton, Exford or Simonsbath. There are youth hostels at Lynton, Exford and on the high edge of the moors above Minehead.

Quantocks

A few miles to the east of Exmoor lie the Quantock Hills, a 3-mile wide ridge running from the Vale of Taunton to the coast near Watchet. Very Exmoor-like in character, with rounded summits and bracken-clad slopes, pierced by wooded combes. The best walk is surely the breezy prehistoric track along the ridge, leading to superb views at Beacon Hill above the Quantoxhead villages, most easily reached at Triscombe Stone or Park Gate above Crowcombe. The Quantocks are explored from the villages tucked below the hills—Crowcombe or Holford—both of which have nearby youth hostels.

Bodmin Moor

This smaller version of Dartmoor is usually missed by those hurrying towards the attractions of the Cornish coast. The best of the moor lies north of the one crossing road—the bleak granite-strewn tops of Brown Willy (1,377ft) and the National Trust's Rough Tor (1,311ft), pronounced to rhyme with 'now'. All around are the stones and hut circles of prehistoric settlement. The easiest approach will be the lane up from Camelford, and explorers will probably be staying in one of the coast resorts.

Brecon Beacons and Black Mountains

The Old Red Sandstone of the Brecon Beacons forms the most

southerly upland group of Wales, rising from the very head of the desecrated mining valleys. Furthest west of the mountain groups within the National Park area is Black Mountain (the *single* one), rising to its highest point in Carmarthen Van (2,460ft). Then comes Fforest Fawr, a series of peaks culminating in Fan Fawr (2,409ft), divided only by the steep-sided valley of the Brecon to Merthyr road from the great multiple ridge of the Brecon Beacons. Highest point is the 2,906ft peak of Pen y Fan, whence the precipitous carved-out cwms and ridges fall away northwards to Brecon. Then, eastward of the Usk valley, the Black Mountains (plural this time) rise in a series of ridges like an outstretched hand, all around the 2,000ft contour. All these areas provide fine easy ridge walks—the great horseshoe of the Beacons themselves, or the sandstone ridges of the Black Mountains divided by such lush broad valleys as the Vale of Ewyas, with Llanthony Priory superbly placed in it. The Monmouth and Brecon Canal towpath, following just above the River Usk, provides an unusually level valley walk with views of the hills; and for the joy of tumbling water, explore the waterfall country around Ystradfellte, where streams drop down from the heights of Fforest Fawr. Brecon is the best centre for the Beacons, a clear way leading to the summit ridge above Cwm Cymwyn; and Crickhowell, Hay-on-Wye or Abergavenny (with its paths up over the Sugar Loaf), for the Black Mountains. Llandovery is best for the Carmarthen peaks. There are youth hostels at Crickhowell, Capel-y-Ffin in Ewyas Vale, Ty'n-y-Caeau near Brecon, Llwyn-y-Celyn beneath the Beacons, Llanddeusant beneath Carmarthen Van, and Ystradfellte amid the waterfalls.

Shropshire Hills

In the south-west of the county several lines of hills run in almost parallel lines diagonally across the map, providing with their geological diversity a very wide range of walks. The rift valley of Church Stretton lies at the heart, with the Long Mynd, a moorland top reaching the 1,700ft mark, rising steeply to one side. The best known paths follow the Cardingmill valley up to the summit and ancient Port Way. Westward of the Long Mynd further craggy ridges rise to the Stiperstones, crowned by weird rock formations. On the other side of the Church Stretton valley come first the Stretton Hills, volcanic rock reaching its climax in the prominent Caer Caradoc (1,506ft), and then, beyond the broad Ape Dale, the long wooded line of Wenlock Edge, where Housman-lovers can look over familiar scenes as 'the gale, it plies the saplings double'. The Stretton villages are the obvious centres for exploring, plus youth hostels at Bridges in the Ratlinghope valley and Wilderhope Manor high on Wenlock Edge.

Central Wales

Much of the central Welsh upland is rather featureless moor with a considerable portion afforested or drowned by reservoirs. But the Plynlimon range rises above the area around as a vast plateau reaching its summit with Pen Plynlimon Fawr at 2,468ft. Because the surrounding moor is high, views are not spectacular. Well used paths lead up from the main Aberystwyth road above Ponterwyd. This village, with nearby Devil's Bridge, provide the best centres for walking not only the Plynlimon group but also the paths in the beautiful wooded gorge of the Rheidol. Devil's Bridge has spectacular falls where the Rheidol and Mynach rivers join, and also the terminus of a still-operating narrow gauge railway that climbs up from Aberystwyth. There is a useful youth hostel in the hamlet of Ystumtuen, near Ponterwyd.

Snowdonia

Second only to the Lake District in the range and extent of its mountains, the Snowdonia National Park covers 845 square miles of north-west Wales and encompasses a wider area than the surroundings of Snowdon itself. These ranges are vast and craggy folds of ancient rock, offering in places the most testing faces for experienced rock climbers; indeed mountain centres such as Pen-y-Gwryd are written copiously into the pages of mountaineering history. Some cliffs are sheer, and some mountain ways too difficult or exposed for the average walker, so it is best to keep to the many well used paths. Remember that even these can be treacherous under snow or ice; every year sees its crop of accidents as inexperienced venturers overestimate their ability to tackle Snowdonia in winter conditions.

The old compressed rock has resulted in the vast slate quarries of Dinorwic and Blaenau Ffestiniog, while glaciation is revealed with superb effect in such U-shaped valleys as Nant Ffrancon, and the vast basins or cwms scooped by ice action from the slopes of Snowdon and Cader Idris. The valley mouths as they near the sea have flooded to form some of our very finest estuary landscapes—Mawddach and Dovey in particular—while inland the tranquil lake of Tal-y-llyn, reflecting Cader Idris, shows the breathtaking beauty of water in a glaciated valley.

Eryri, 'the eagles' nesting place', is the poetically appropriate Welsh name for these mountains, and hardly anywhere else can the walker explore such scenes of awe-inspiring majesty. There are still some lingering problems of access, but none that will be encountered by considerate users of the recognised walking routes. Do not be distracted by the county practice of using the Welsh 'Llwybr Cyhoeddus' on one face of each public footpath sign. It means the same. As in the Lakes, the youth hostels are plentiful enough to enable valley to valley tours to be planned in diversity; there are some fifteen hostels in the National Park and another four just beyond the boundaries. The area is best described in mountain groups, from south to north.

Cader Idris. Between the estuaries of the Mawddach and Dovey rises the majestic 2,927ft peak of Cader Idris, probably the most popular ascent after Snowdon, for its views and the many ways up from either side. The line of high ground rises from the coast for several miles, giving an easy grassy walk to the summit, where rocky spurs lead southward, one of them enclosing the superb cwm that holds the dark water of Llyn Cau. To the north another hollow, the 'chair' of Idris, holds another lake—Llyn y Gadair. The near views are dramatic, and the distant views superb to the Mawddach estuary and beyond to the sea. The best known routes up are from a $\frac{1}{2}$ mile above Tal-y-llyn from the south, or by the Foxes Path on the Dolgellau side. On a fine day no walker will resist the ridge walk westwards, with several easy slopes to drop down on. From Barmouth a shorter walk across the estuary footbridge to the National Trust's Llynnau Cregennen provides mountain tarns in meadows plus a fine view of the north face of Cader. Centres comprise Dolgellau, Barmouth, or Tal-y-llyn, and there is a well placed youth hostel, Kings, at the foot of Foxes Path.

Rhinogs. Some of the wildest terrain in the country is spanned by this group of craggy and impressive mountains, forming the crest of the 'Harlech Dome'. Along a north-south line that rises from Barmouth are four major peaks—Diffwys (2,462ft), Y Llethr (2,475ft), Rhinog Fach (2,333ft) and Rhinog Fawr (2,362ft). From Barmouth northwards for a time this can be treated as a simple ridge walk, but do not be deceived; beyond Y Llethr deep and desolate passes separate each peak. No ridge walk this! First Bwlch Ardudwy separates the two Rhinogs, then comes Bwlch Tyddiad, taking the strange paved way known as Roman Steps, probably medieval in origin. The Rhinogs are tough rocky going, difficult even to reach, but mountain lovers will want at least to approach them, for the grandeur of steep cliffs and remote tarns. These are real mountains; the foothills are best reached via roads and tracks up from Harlech, Llanbedr, Tal-y-bont and other points along the coast road. Barmouth is an attractive centre, with its nearby Panorama Walk for superb views up the estuary. Dolgellau, too, has its Precipice Walk, giving distant panoramic views of the range. There are useful youth hostels at Harlech and Llanbedr.

Moel Siabod Group. To the south-east of the Nant Gwynant road lies a rocky upland area not all that frequented, perhaps because of the greater attractions a few miles to the West. Moel Siabod itself (2,861ft) is an isolated pinnacle of mountain that rises directly above Capel Curig, and easy to climb from that centre up gentle grassy slopes. Standing back as it does, the summit offers a superb view of the Snowdon range. Dropping down, still with grass underfoot, these hills rise again to other summits, with beautiful little Llyn Edno lying beneath Cnicht (2,265ft) and then Moelwyn Mawr (2,527ft). Cnicht, offering equally fine views, can best be climbed by paths leaving the Nanmor valley road; indeed all this area offers attractive walking to anyone staying in Beddgelert at one end of the range or Capel Curig at the other, or at the youth hostels at Bryn Gwynant or Pont-y-pant in the Lledr valley.

Snowdon Massif. Dominating all others in its height and popularity, Snowdon (3,560ft) has the distinction of being the highest point in England and Wales. This doubtless is why on a summer's day over 1,000 people will set out for the top, on foot or via the mountain railway that leads up to a refreshment house just beneath the summit. In fine weather they will be rewarded by dramatic views all round, but lovers of solitude will reserve Snowdon for an early spring or autumn day.

There are routes up from all sides, all of them clearly defined. Pen-y-pass is the most popular starting point, mainly because it already stands 1,169ft up. The easy Miners Track leaves the car park to climb gently via Llyn Teyrn, Llyn Llydaw and Glaslyn, eventually to join the famous Pyg Track as it begins its zigzag pull up to the summit ridge. The Pyg Track also begins from Pen-y-pass, but erosion caused by many tramping feet has led to its diversion currently to a route that climbs first up the left side of Llanberis pass. On the shoulder of Bwlch y Moch paths divide, the left-hand Pyg Track continuing upwards above the lakes to its zigzag scree climb to the summit; the right-hand path leads more steeply and directly on to Crib Goch, to follow this narrow ridge to the summit. This ridge scramble is the beginning of the 'Snowdon Horseshoe', climbing to Yr Wyddfa, then taking Y Lliwedd as the other arm of the shoe.

Longest but least arduous way up is the Llanberis Path, following one side or other of the mountain railway, and an easily graded 5-mile walk. The highest climb, in theory at least, is the Watkin Path, starting a mere 200ft above sea level in Nant Gwynant. It begins at the car park by Pont Bethania, climbing gradually but continuously up Cwm y Llan until it turns right for its steep scramble up the shoulder of Y Lliwedd. Knowing the rough condition of this path, discerning walkers turn left instead to approach the summit via Bwlch Main. Yet another track ascends from near Beddgelert via Ffridduchaf Farm up to the Llechog ridge, with fine views. Probably the oldest route of all, Snowdon Ranger, leaves the shores of Llyn Cwellyn just to the

Walkers prepare to climb the Pyg Track, best-known of routes up Snowdon. Beyond them, the spectacular pass of Llanberis

left of the youth hostel to zigzag up the slopes of Clogwyn du'r Arddu to the summit. Beddgelert, Rhyd-ddu, Llanberis and Pen-y-Gwryd are all obvious centres for the Snowdon climb, as are youth hostels at Llanberis, Pen-y-pass, Bryn Gwynant and Snowdon Ranger.

The Glyders. Facing the Snowdon massif across Llanberis pass lies the Glyder range, with a southern aspect of steep grassy slopes contrasting vividly with a succession of dramatic cwms on the northern side. From Capel Curig the range rises westward in a succession of peaks, Glyder Fach (3,262ft), Glyder Fawr (3,279ft) and Y Garn (3,104ft), with the fine outriding peak of Tryfan (3,010ft) towering above Llyn Ogwen. The ridge walk up from Capel Curig is a long excursion, and it is from Llyn Ogwen that most walkers will start out—from Ogwen Cottage, the mountain centre, or nearby Idwal Cottage, a youth hostel. Paths lead directly upward to skirt Llyn Idwal and scramble to the ridge

126

by the aptly named Devil's Kitchen, or to follow the old miners' track by Llyn Bochlwyd and over to Pen-y-Gwryd. Tryfan in its splendid isolation attracts many mountain lovers, but the summit can only be reached by an energetic though hardly dangerous scramble, either up the north face from the head of Llyn Ogwen or from the southern shoulder where the miners' track crosses. Hardly footpath walking!

Carneddau. To the north of the Ogwen valley and the great Nant Ffrancon below it lies the most northerly mountain group in Wales, the Carneddau. A vast area of grassy ridges and rocky outcrops, this is interesting open country to walk over, but the great distances to be covered make an expedition across the Carneddau a venture for experienced walkers only. Landmarks are few, and expert map and compass work is needed, to arrive when and where intended. The main summits are Carnedd Llywelyn (3,484ft) and Carnedd Dafydd (3,426ft), both reached most easily from the head of Llyn Ogwen. But probably for most walkers the gentle foothills behind Capel Curig will hold the most attraction. The path up a wild valley from the village over to Llyn Crafnant is a 'must' and the easy diversion on to Clogwyn Mawr gives fine views up the two branching valleys to Snowdon and to the Glyders. The centres are clearly Ogwen and Capel Curig, both with hostels, and there is another youth hostel at Ro Wen on the Roman road that crosses the northern corner of the area.

Forest of Bowland and Pendle Hill

Bowland, once a hunting forest and never tree-covered as the name might suggest, is a broad area of gritstone moorland rising to the 1,800ft mark in the north-west of Lancashire. Roads are few, only one crossing the centre through the Trough of Bowland. As rough grazing and grouse moor, these open hills with their fine views were long denied to ramblers by gamekeepers guarding the grouse, except for a very few and well used rights of way. But recently several access agreements have been made after years of pressure. Near Lancaster, over 1,700 acres of Clougha Moor are now open and Clougha Pike, once reached by one solitary footpath, can be explored from several access points. Further south, another 1,000 acres of Fair Snape Fell and Saddle Fell offer open access, reached by pleasant paths from Chipping village or Bleasdale. Notice boards locally give details of access points, and in fact there are other moorland areas where by tradition you will be able to walk without likelihood of being stopped.

Pendle Hill (1,831ft) is a detached viewpoint, a well known landmark and favourite excursion for many living in nearby towns, via tracks up from Barley or Downham. It shares many features with both the Bowland fells to the north-west and the Pennines to the east. Centres for this area are Slaidburn, Lancaster, Longridge and Clitheroe, with a youth hostel at Slaidburn. To the north centres such as Clapham or the Ingleton youth hostel are well placed for exploring Bowland and the Yorkshire Dales National Park.

9 Deep in the Rural Scene

No other country in the world can offer such a variety of scenery within small compass as our own, and we would be missing a great deal of rich experience if we were to confine our walking to the high hills. This chapter sets out to introduce some of the other landscapes, each with its own distinctive character. Most of the areas selected have been designated as Areas of Outstanding Natural Beauty, by the Countryside Commission. Today there are over thirty such areas, where special efforts are made by the county council to keep unwanted development out and to retain the character of the landscape, its farming use and wild life.

In most cases they are too small as distinctive areas to form National Parks, the more ambitious designation, but within their more modest span they can offer as high a scenic value, and their small-scale landscapes may be even better suited to a quiet walk. Two other areas reviewed, the New Forest and the Forest of Dean, are administered by the Forestry Commission, the latter being designated a Forest Park. Within these forests the Commission, our largest landholder, provides free access and such other simple facilities for enjoying them as parking and picnic places, viewpoints and waymarked forest trails.

In many of these areas the beauty is not that of wild country but of a more domesticated man-made scene. Access to them on foot will be via their network of footpaths and bridleways, and fortunately the upsurge of interest in walking has led to the production of many booklets describing footpath walks by local experts. Almost every area we describe will be served by these helpful little publications, which you are most likely to find in local shops.

As with the hill country, we follow a clockwise course around the country.

Yorkshire Wolds

Geographically the Yorkshire Wolds rise gently from the fore-shore of the Humber Estuary to reach a northern escarpment overlooking the Vale of Pickering. Much of the character of the area comes from the valleys that run in a narrow crescent from Ferriby in the south, through to Pocklington, Thixendale and Settrington, to meet the ridge, which itself is indented with narrow valleys as it reaches north-eastward to the sea at Filey.

Until World War I the Wolds were almost entirely sheep grazing. Now only the narrow dales remain untouched by the plough and they offer the best Wolds' walking today. Few roads penetrate the dales, hence much of their charm. Rather than sweeping prospects, they have the fascination of concealing what lies around the next bend as you follow them on their twisting, almost secret, courses.

A good centre for exploring them is Pocklington on the Wolds' southern edge. Other villages are small and scattered, although there is plenty of evidence in deserted villages that this region was once well peopled. Most notable of the deserted village sites is Wharram Percy, and a visit there could be coupled with a walk along the right of way above the old Burdale railway tunnel, one of the longest and most dangerous of all to build. There is a summer-only youth hostel at Thixendale, and other hostels at Malton and Scarborough.

White Peak

The southern half of the Peak District National Park, known as the White Peak for its limestone composition, offers more relaxed and sheltered walking than the high moors of the Dark Peak. The limestone plateau, with its pastureland divided by drystone walls, is dissected by deep valleys carrying clear streams that rise near Buxton to flow generally southward. All offer superb footpath walking. The Derbyshire Wye flows through Chee Dale and Miller's Dale, spectacular limestone gorges in places, then turns through exquisite Monsal Dale. The Manifold has its own fine twisting dale, with caves and a length that bafflingly vanishes

The path through Dovedale in the White Peak crosses the Dove
by Viator's Bridge to the little hamlet of Milldale

under the limestone near Ilam. The Dove, best known of all,
flows down through craggy Wolfscote Dale, beneath the pinnacles
and caves of Mill Dale and Dovedale itself. From Thorpe Cloud
up to Hartington is one of the finest walks in the land. Explore
the area from Buxton, Matlock or Ashbourne, or from youth
hostels at Ilam, Hartington, Buxton, Ravenstor in Miller's Dale,
and a whole string in the Wye and Derwent valleys. For an
equally easy high walk try the Tissington Trail, 11 miles of grass
track with waymarked walks leading off, from Mapleton to
Hartington along an old railway line.

Chiltern Hills

Folded chalk hills to the north-west of London, the Chilterns
have their own unmistakeable character—a succession of long
ridges and 'bottoms' falling away southwards from the high

northern escarpment. The valleys are usually open and dry, the ridge-tops crowned by great beechwoods that flourish on the clay layer on top of the chalk, superb in autumn. Good, well preserved little villages, such as Hambledon, Turville, Fingest, Bradenham, and Aldbury, flourish in their vales. All are watched over vigilantly by the energetic Chiltern Society and its Footpath Group, which tends what must surely be the finest network of rural paths anywhere—well walked, signposted, and often waymarked as well. Most Chiltern walkers will be Londoners, and communications are good to points like Chesham, Amersham or Wendover on the old Metropolitan line, or to Berkhamsted or Tring, High Wycombe or Princes Risborough, Marlow or Henley on other lines. For introductory walks try the Hambledon valley north from the village, the delectable little Chess Valley around Chenies, the escarpment walk west from Wendover over Coombe Hill, or the autumn beechwoods of Ashridge, reached over Berkhamsted Common.

Surrey Hills

South of London the chalk rises gradually to form the almost continuous escarpment of the North Downs. From Hog's Back, via Box Hill, Colley Hill and many other familiar viewpoints, it extends to the Kent border and far beyond, sometimes open, sometimes wooded. On the back of the chalk, sandy pockets have formed the characteristic Surrey commons, Ockham, Wisley and others. A far-sighted county council has for many years been acquiring these valuable 'lungs', and today a series of open spaces also follow the North Downs summit line—Newlands Corner, Netley Heath, White Downs and others—along with the National Trust's Ranmore Common, Headley Heath, Reigate Hill etc. Thus Londoners have many areas where they can walk freely along the downs, from popular starting points like Guildford or Newlands Corner, Dorking or Box Hill. A parallel line of greensand just a few miles south of the chalk rises to the higher

Ramblers on the Kent/Surrey border take the path that links
Ide Hill in the background with Toys Hill, following the line of the
greensand hills

Pitch, Holmbury and Leith Hills, the last at 965ft being the highest spot in south-east England. Again the high heathlands are public open spaces, with free walking over sandy paths through pine and birch woods. In the south-east corner of the county the greensand rises around Haslemere to form the great amphitheatre of Devil's Punchbowl and the sand-ringed ponds of Frensham Common, all National Trust open land.

South Downs

Beyond the weald the chalk rises again in the 70-mile line of the South Downs—smooth whaleback hills reaching 800ft in height —which start in Hampshire to march across Sussex and end at the Seven Sisters and Beachy Head, soaring 534ft cliffs near Eastbourne. The downs are cut through by four rivers—Cuckmere, Ouse, Adur and Arun—on their way to the Channel. West of the Arun the hills are mainly wooded, with such occasional viewpoints as Bignor Hill, Cocking Down or Beacon Hill. Eastward are the open downs, traditional sheep-grazings of the chalk, with great bowls of valleys cut into the escarpment. In recent years much land has been brought under the plough and the sheep are fewer; paths that once crossed open grassy downland are now fenced. But much good breezy walking remains, along the northern escarpment with its views, or on the ancient tracks that follow the ridges southward. The downs attract many visitors from the big coast resorts of Brighton, Worthing and Eastbourne, but, for pleasanter access—choose the centres that nestle beneath the scarp, Alfriston, Lewes, Bramber, Steyning, Storrington, or Arundel in the Arun gap.

Isle of Wight

This area has great geological interest, where the walker will set his eyes immediately to the fine chalk downland, and then to the southern coast. A sharp upfold of the chalk begins at the Needles and runs right across the island. An excellent ridge walk begins at Shorwell and comes right to the sea at Freshwater Bay, continuing on to the Needles over Tennyson Down. Another, broader, band of chalk provides more breezy walking above the sea behind Ventnor, rising to 785ft on St Boniface Down. In complete contrast, very interesting walks from Ventnor explore the Landslip and its tangled woodland just above the sea, and follow the undercliff for miles round to Blackgang Chine. The chines, great ravines leading down through the cliffs to beach Lymington River and Black Water. Other centres are Cadnam, in holiday months, but the island closes down out of season!

New Forest

Since the forest dates from Norman times, it is hardly 'new'. Today over 100 square miles are administered by the Forestry Commission. It is not formally a Forest Park; its status is defined by Acts of Parliament that establish the rights of commoners and the powers of the ancient Verderers Court, but facilities for visitors are provided as they would be in a Park. Half the area is wild open heathland, a plateau reaching 414ft on Longcross Plain, and the rest is woodland still in its ancient enclosures. The semi-wild New Forest ponies, which are owned by the commoners and rounded up each year, help to keep the grazings clear. There are herds of deer, too, but not so easy to find. Walking is easy, but many areas can get boggy underfoot, and there is great scope for getting lost, especially in the forest rides. Lyndhurst is the recognised centre for exploring, with nearby Brockenhurst equally well placed, particularly for walks up the Lymington River and Black Water. Other centres are Cadnam, Ringwood and Beaulieu; a fascinating walk from the last-named leads by the Beaulieu River to Bucklers Hard, where forest oaks were once turned into ships of the line. There are youth hostels at Norleywood nearby, and at Burley.

Wessex Downs

Our finest chalk upland area, in Berkshire, Wiltshire and also entering Hampshire, is often known as the Wessex Downs. From the Thames Valley at Goring the northern escarpment swings in a great 40-mile curve above the Vale of White Horse, the

Lambourn Downs, and then the Marlborough Downs. Southward the chalk uplands are split by the Lambourn and Kennet Vales, before coming to a fine high south-facing escarpment above the Vale of Pewsey, with Milk Hill reaching 964ft. Beyond, the downs rise again to form the high plateau of Salisbury Plain, much taken over by the military, but further east above Hungerford they rise to their highest point of all at Inkpen Beacon, 974ft. These high downlands rose securely above the forests even in prehistoric times, and the traces of ancient settlement are everywhere. The old Ridgeway track follows the northern scarp, providing fine walking past the Iron Age hill forts of Segsbury, Uffington, Liddington and Barbury, and past chambered barrows and the great stone circle of Avebury. Above Pewsey Vale it meets the Wansdyke, an equally early earthwork. Indeed, everywhere you walk over the Wessex Downs you will be following in ancient footsteps along prehistoric tracks and Roman roads. Marlborough is an ideal centre, with downland and horse-gallops on three sides, and the majestic avenues of old Savernake Forest on the fourth. Newbury, Devizes and Wantage are other centres, but the one youth hostel within reach is at Streatley.

Purbeck and Dorset Coast

The Isle of Purbeck (no island!) provides both downland and coast walks within a very small area. A narrow line of uplifted chalk provides the ridge walk along the Purbeck Hills, broken dramatically by the gap guarded by old Corfe Castle. The ridge comes to the sea over Ballard Down, the chalk ending in Old Harry Rocks. Westward beyond Swanage the cliff path follows the finest unspoilt coastline in the south, first above the strange Dancing Ledge (almost at sea level), then over St Alban's Head to the dark slate of Chapman's Pool. Beyond Kimmeridge a firing range denies access for 6 miles, until one reaches superb Lulworth Cove, where the sea has broken through the Purbeck Limestone to scoop out a perfect semicircle of bay. Beyond come the natural arch of Durdle Door and the towering 500ft chalk headland of White Nothe. Inland the Dorset heaths can be explored over wild tracks from Dorchester, via the great triple earth ramparts of Maiden Castle to the viewpoint of Black Down above Portesham, where the monument to Nelson's Hardy stands at the 777ft mark. Abbotsbury, a pretty village in the foothills by the coast, is popular for its swannery and for the views from nearby modest summits along the Chesil Beach. The main centres are Swanage and Weymouth on the coast, Wareham and Dorchester inland, and there are youth hostels at Swanage and Litton Cheney.

Mendips

Rising from the Somerset levels, the long line of the Mendip Hills forms a high limestone plateau cut deeply in places by steep-sided gorges, Cheddar being the best known. Underground streams, working away at the limestone, have formed the complex cave systems at Cheddar and Wookey, now, alas, surrounded by all the trappings of tourist attractions! On top the plateau is a bleak landscape of stone-walled fields, offering little scope for walking. You had best take the track up from Cheddar over to Black Down (1,067ft), where there are open paths galore and fine views to the Bristol Channel; or find the paths high on either side of Cheddar Gorge, to look down on the milling mortals below and carry on up a wild valley to remote Charterhouse, with intriguing remains of the old lead-mining communities all around. Escape the crowds at Wookey Hole by taking the waymarked paths up to the nature reserve of Ebbor Gorge. The centres are Wells and Cheddar, the latter having a youth hostel.

Cotswolds

North from Bath runs the line of the Cotswold Hills, a high limestone escarpment looking over the Severn Vale, and dipping gently away to the south-east. The upland areas present a farming landscape of neat stone walls and old hedgerows, but in the better known northern half are the gentle valleys of streams that wander down to the Thames, Coln, Leach, Windrush and Evenlode. Also the most delectable villages and market towns in the world, built in the creamy-grey Cotswold limestone, built on

A shady walk through a Douglas Fir plantation in the Forest
of Dean, typical of many walks provided by the Forestry
Commission

the prosperity of the wool industry, which thrived here into the sixteenth century. Chipping Campden with its open market hall, Bibury with its enchanting row of wool-workers' cottages, the Slaughter villages, Naunton, Stanton or Stanway—everyone will want to make their own 'most beautiful' award. Walking 'over the top' will mainly be on the old farm tracks, for there are relatively few footpaths. Most ramblers will want to follow the valleys and explore the villages, the walk down the Coln from Coln St Dennis to Coln St Aldwyns via Ablington and Bibury being perhaps the best. However, points on the north escarpment do provide open walking—over Cleeve Common to Cleeve Cloud, for example, the highest point in the Cotswolds at 1,083ft. Centres for the northern Cotswolds are Stow-on-the-Wold, Broadway, Moreton-in-Marsh, Cheltenham, Bourton-on-the-Water, Burford, Cirencester and Lechlade, with youth hostels at Stow-on-the-Wold, Cleeve Hill and Duntisbourne Abbotts.

Wye Valley and Forest of Dean

From Ross-on-Wye the River Wye flows in a series of great loops down to the Severn by Chepstow. One of its early loops takes it beneath the fine viewpoint of Symonds Yat Rock. Beyond Monmouth its vale grows ever narrower, with steep lime-stone cliffs and gorges, and the ruined Tintern Abbey on its valley floor. Offa's Dyke Path provides a good walk, usually high above the river, up to Monmouth, whence equally delightful riverside paths continue upstream. To the east lies the high plateau of the ancient Royal Forest of Dean—rolling country, still richly wooded, with a fine variety of oak, beech, ash and conifers. Speech House near Cannop is the traditional centre of the Forest, and meeting place of the Verderers Court. Today this area is a National Forest Park to which the Forestry Commission allows free access, but over this maze of tracks and paths it is all too easy to get lost. Aware of this, the Ramblers' Association has for many years maintained a series of waymarked paths around Speech House and in Highmeadow Woods behind Symonds Yat, and the Forestry Commission's nature trails provide shorter walks in the same areas. Leaflets are available locally.

The youth hostels at Mitcheldean and St Briavels castle are linked by a 14-mile waymarked route right across the forest. There are also hostels at Chepstow and Welsh Bicknor on the Wye, and other accommodation at Chepstow, Monmouth, Symonds Yat and Cinderford.

Gower Peninsula

A miraculously preserved oasis of fine scenery on the industrialised coast of South Wales, Gower offers a combination of high downland and fine coastal walking. From Mumbles Head to Worms Head the coast path leads by strangely tilted cliffs created by limestone formations, wide sandy inlets and long curves of dune and beach. It is an exhilarating walk, even including a couple of modest estuaries to wade across. Beyond Worms Head, a nature reserve, lies broad Rhossili Bay, and from there onwards the north coast of the peninsula, in total contrast, is low sand and marsh. The sandstone Rhossili Downs rise almost direct from the sea, and the long back of Cefn y Bryn provides bird's-eye views of the craggy coastline and distant views northward over Burry Inlet. Swansea and Mumbles are the big centres, but, for the real taste of the sea, try the youth hostel at Port Eynon—a converted lifeboat house right on the beach.

Arnside and Silverdale

Tucked away on the approaches to the Lake District, and passed by multitudes hurrying that way along the M6 or the coast line to Grange and Ulverston, the Arnside and Silverdale area offers plenty of interest to the explorer on foot. A small-scale landscape of modest wooded limestone hills contrasts with the tidal estuary of the Kent and Morecambe Bay—wide expanses of sand and mud at low tide, swiftly covered by the incoming waters. From little Arnside Knott (500ft) there are fine views over the bay to the distant Coniston fells. The estuary and the marshy low valleys or 'mosses' attract bird life, and Leighton Moss is a national wildfowl sanctuary. The villages of Arnside, Silverdale and Milnthorpe give access to extensive footpaths; there is a youth hostel at Arnside.

10 The Longer Walks

As well as exploring the complex network of public paths in the country, today the walker has a growing number of long-distance routes he can follow. These link and extend the existing paths to enable continuous journeys to be made on foot, often over the finest countryside, far from the roar of traffic. The routes offer varying degrees of challenge, from a pleasant weekend's outing to a rugged 3-week expedition that truly tests powers of endurance. They often follow the natural lines of river, hill crest or escarpment; put prehistoric ways to an appropriate new use; or link logical points to give the walker an objective worth attaining at the end of his journey.

Their attraction is not limited to the hardy walker with time to spare. It is perfectly practical to follow short lengths of these routes as the basis of a day's outing; quite a high proportion of their users are doing just this. Some routes can be tackled as a succession of separate outings, gradually linking together until the whole line is completed.

The concept of a long-distance walk was first advocated in this country by Tom Stephenson, secretary of the Ramblers' Association from 1948 to 1969. In a newspaper article in 1935 he proposed a 'long green trail', a Pennine Way from the Peak to the Cheviots that would, in our own modest way, emulate the 2,000-mile Appalachian Trail in the eastern states of America. Tom continued to campaign, even taking parties of MPs to walk parts of his embryo Pennine Way. The idea attracted considerable interest and led to the formation of a Pennine Way Association. Finally, in 1949, the National Parks and Access to the Countryside Act set up a National Parks Commission and charged it with suggesting long-distance routes and implementing any proposals approved by the appropriate Minister.

Naturally enough the ready surveyed Pennine Way was the first proposal, submitted in June 1951. Within 15 days the Minister approved it and sent a note round to authorities expressing the hope that new rights of way would be speedily created so that the route might be open by Easter 1952. He was over-optimistic. The Pennine Way was not finally opened until 1965, 30 years after it was first suggested. The National Parks Commission and its successor the Countryside Commission have opened several other routes since that date, eight routes now providing around 1,500 miles of walking. Most delays have resulted from problems in trying to fill gaps in the existing path system, to avoid the need for road walking. Local authorities have the duty to negotiate with landowners for the necessary new rights of way, but have tried to get results by agreement rather than by compulsion.

The 'Unofficial' Routes

Meanwhile many other long-distance walks have been devised by ramblers, using the existing paths. Some of these are intended eventually to gain official recognition by the Countryside Commission, while others, mainly the shorter routes, have been adopted by their respective county councils. All offer considerable advantages to the walker, as experienced ramblers have planned and surveyed them to follow the best route, and in most cases work has gone into improving the paths with new footbridges, signposting and waymarking to prepare them for greater use. As it would not be possible to follow any such planned route without a description to guide you, some form of publication is always available. In this book we have tried to indicate where to get these guides, but in an ever-changing situation it is useful to know that the Ramblers' Association can supply a free 'Fact Sheet' listing the latest long-distance path information.

It is important to distinguish between the 'official' Countryside Commission routes and others. You will find the Commission's routes signposted in their own way—either an oak signpost with the name of the way in raised letters or a low concrete plinth with the name cast in. At other points where the route may be in doubt waymarks may also be provided; the acorn symbol denotes a long-distance route, either as a metal plaque fastened to gateposts or fences, or stencilled on to a tree, stone wall or

The acorn waymark of the Countryside Commission on the Pennine Way, which climbs to the left of the cliffs of Malham Cove, beyond

boulder. These are intended to help but in no way to substitute for a good map. Waymarks can be worn away, trees fall, plaques mysteriously vanish, so never rely too heavily on them. The official routes have, in the main, been walked for long enough now to be well trodden ways even in open country, but again do not expect anything extra by way of surfacing; they remain rough tracks.

On the Pennine Way in particular mapboards have been sited at intervals, mainly as a check for you if you carry an unmarked map. In fact, if your map is a new 1:50,000 scale sheet, it will probably show the long-distance route, labelled at intervals. One further advantage in the well established official long-distance route is that it will have encouraged more accommodation along its line. Several new youth hostels have been opened to serve the Pennine Way, and many a remote shepherd's cottage will now provide a welcome overnight stop to bridge a long gap. With this in mind, 'where to stay' guides are published for several of the routes.

It is worth remembering that most of these routes, official and unofficial, have been created simply by linking existing paths. This is something that everyone can do, with a map and an urge

right: On the plateau of Cross Fell the Pennine Way reaches its highest point, then follows the ridges to Great Dun Fell in the distance

One of the Pennine Way mapboards at Middleton in Teesdale

to try an unusual journey. There is no need to walk only where other enthusiasts have tramped out a route for you. Try, perhaps without any serious intent, planning your own expedition for a weekend or a week, using the paths that lead you through the best country with the least road walking. Perhaps the greatest value in these existing ways is to whet the appetite for the kind of adventurous journey we have almost forgotten how to make.

These are the official routes.

Pennine Way

Still the best known of the long-distance walks, the Pennine Way has attracted a steadily increasing number of walkers since its opening. The Way, in following the Pennine chain, passes through much of the finest country en route, and through three National Parks. It starts at Edale in the Peak District and traverses the moorland in the north of the National Park before descending to cross the Calder valley near Hebden Bridge. After passing through Brontë country the Way briefly follows the Leeds and Liverpool Canal before reaching Gargrave and following the Aire to Malham in the Yorkshire Dales. Beyond Malham village the Way visits the famous Cove and Tarn before heading over the moors to climb Penyghent, one of the Three Peaks. The Way continues through the National Park before striking north over Stainmore and on to Teesdale. The upper Tees is followed for

several miles past High Force and Cauldron Snout, beyond which a westerly track leads to High Cup Nick and thence down to the Eden valley at Dufton. Returning to the fells, the Way traverses Cross Fell, at 2,930ft the highest point on its route. The general line of the South Tyne valley is then taken to Hadrian's Wall, and its most spectacular section is followed for several miles. The fringes of the vast Kielder Forest are traversed in the walk on to Bellingham and Byrness, beyond which the Cheviots are covered in a final 25-mile trek, with an extra 2-mile option to the top of Cheviot itself, ending at Kirk Yetholm just over the Scottish border.

The success of the Way has not made the walk any less strenuous, and it remains, as intended, an extremely demanding 250 miles. Much of the route lies well over the 1,000ft contour, where weather conditions are unpredictable and sometimes unpleasant. In poor weather moorland heights like Kinder, Bleaklow, Black Hill, White Moss, Great Shunner Fell, Cross Fell or the Cheviots should not be attempted by anyone unfamiliar with map and compass work; indeed, even the most experienced walkers will avoid the heights on some days. But given fair conditions the Way should not present difficulties to reasonably good walkers.

Most wayfarers devote 3 weeks to the full walk, which timetable provides for several rest days. There are youth hostels on or near the route at Edale, Crowden, Marsden, Mankinholes,

Earby, Malham, Stainforth, Hawes, Keld, Langdon Beck, Dufton, Alston, Once Brewed, Bellingham, Byrness and Kirk Yetholm.

Some stretches of the Pennine Way lend themselves to shorter walks that explore the highlights. *From Edale* the alternative 'bad weather' route can be taken via Upper Booth, Jacob's Ladder and Edale Cross, then along the escarpment to Kinder Downfall. The adventurous could then return via Kinder River across the summit to descent Grindsbrook. *From Malham village* the Way climbs to the left of Malham Cove, over limestone pavements to Malham Tarn, whence a return could be made via Gordale Beck and the steep spectacular drop down Gordale Scar. *From Horton in Ribblesdale* follow the Way up Horton Scar Lane to climb with it over Penyghent, returning to Horton by turning right at Churn Milk Hole. *From Thwaite in Swaledale* take the Way northwards high above the Swale to Keld. Explore the several waterfalls, then cross the river and return on the other bank via Muker village. *From Middleton in Teesdale* take the Way (which almost enters the village) as it follows the Tees past Low Force to High Force, a beautiful 5-mile river walk. *From Greenhead* on the A69 pick up the Way as it crosses the Gilsland Road and follow it eastwards via Thirlwall Castle along the Roman Wall via Walltown Crags, Winshields and above Crag Lough to House-steads Fort. Pause before Cuddy's Crags to look northward, where the Pennine Way goes now, into the vast Border Forests. This 9-mile walk can be much shortened if you pick it up above Twice-Brewed Inn on the B6318.

Cleveland Way

The second long-distance route opened, the Cleveland Way, offers two types of walking in almost equal proportions. The route turns in a great arc around the North York Moors National Park, with, first, moorland scenery and fine distant views over the Vale of York, then an impressive walk along some of the highest cliffs of the east coast.

From the market town of Helmsley the route passes Rievaulx Abbey, then climbs to the escarpment of the Hambledon Hills at

Sutton Bank, to follow the old drove road northward above Gormire Lake. Pulling over Black Hambledon, the Way drops down to Osmotherley, then on to the moorland edge again, descending for the Scugdale Beck but rising once more to reach Hasty Bank. Along this stretch the Lyke Wake Walk follows the same route. Northwards now around Greenhow Moor, the Way follows the escarpment of the Cleveland Hills down to Kildale village. Up and on, past the distinctive hill of Roseberry Topping and away north-eastward over the last moorland of Gisborough, it comes down to the coast at Saltburn. Taking the coast path, the Way climbs over high Boulby Cliff into delightful little Staithes, then on to Whitby. Climbing past Whitby Abbey, it continues above cliffs and foreshore with prominent rock formations to Robin Hoods Bay and on to Ravenscar. Beyond Hayburn Wyke the path reaches Scarborough and finally ends just before Filey.

With no vast moorland areas to cross, few navigation problems and heights that never pass the 1,500ft mark, this is clearly less demanding than the Pennine Way. The escarpment can be swept by strong winds, though, so go prepared for the elements. The whole 100-mile walk could be done in an energetic week, but accommodation problems might mean some long stretches of walking around the moorland edge between villages—so best allow longer. The coast stretch, with its popular resorts at Saltburn, Whitby, Robin Hoods Bay, Scarborough and Filey, lends itself to breaking up into relatively short expeditions, and will doubtless be walked this way most often. There are youth hostels at Helmsley, Saltburn, Whitby, Boggle Hole and Scarborough on the Way, and at Westerdale some 3 miles from the route.

Along the moorland edge opportunities for shorter walks on the Cleveland Way occur almost wherever it can be easily reached. *From Helmsley* follow the first 3 miles of the Way up Rye Dale to visit Rievaulx. *From Sutton Bank Top* follow the Way northwards above Gormire Lake. From Osmotherley turn up northwards to follow the Way and Lyke Wake Walk above Arncliffe

overleaf: On the Cleveland Way as it follows the escarpment of the Cleveland Hills, to Hasty Bank and Cringle Moor

Woods, with an attractive diversion down to Mount Grace Priory. *From Kildale* take the Way up on to Great Ayton Moor, then leftward on the path to Roseberry Topping. Along the coast section, there are good accessible cliff walks *from Robin Hoods Bay* to Ravenscar and on to Hayburn Wyke inlet, or *from Staithes* via the old iron-ore quay of Port Mulgrave to Runswick Bay.

North Downs Way

Officially approved but open only in part, the North Downs Way runs from Farnham in Surrey to Dover on the Kent coast, following where possible the crest of the chalk downs. Its line is generally that of the prehistoric route known as the Pilgrims' Way, but whereas the old way kept to the south-facing shoulder of the downs and has in places become a busy road, today's route is usually higher up, for the more open views.

From Farnham the route crosses sandy country beneath the Hog's Back to an old ferry point where a footbridge is proposed to cross the River Wey. Then it runs over the greensand of St Martha's Hill and on to the chalk downs at Newlands Corner to follow the scarp over Box Hill, Colley and Reigate Hills, dropping at the major gaps through the chalk but climbing again over White Hill and Gravelly Hill. At Tatsfield it enters Kent, crossing Chevening Park and the Darent Valley to take the wooded scarp again past Wrotham. Eventually it has to drop for the Medway valley, crossing by footway beside the M2 motorway bridge. Swinging southwards again, it follows the edge of the downs over Bluebell Hill to Hollingbourne, then through orchard country to Wye, just before which an alternative route leaves to go via pretty Chilham to Canterbury and thence to Dover. The main route climbs on to downs again south of Hastingleigh, then via a confused route to Castle Hill and Creteway Down above Folkestone, to follow the cliffs eastward on to Shakespeare Cliff above Dover.

This is the theory. Unfortunately several sections where new rights of way are needed to avoid road walking are still under negotiation. When completed, rambler visitors from France can begin walking as soon as they land. Meanwhile some lengths can be explored with ease, and a 43-mile section between Hollingbourne, Canterbury and Dover was opened in 1972, most of it being the 'Canterbury loop'. All the walking is easy, with no heights above the 700ft line of the downs.

There are opportunities galore for short walks: for example, *from Newlands Corner* over to St Martha's Hill, or eastwards over Netley Heath to Ranmore; or *from Reigate Hill* car park, over Colley Hill and the Buckland Hills. In Kent sample the Way as it sets out *from Hollingbourne* south-eastwards as a rough and ancient trackway; or *from Chilham* take the lane south to Hurst Farm, then the track that leads the Way above Godmersham Park.

South Downs Way

The South Downs face the North Downs across the weald, and along their northern escarpment runs the South Downs Way. Its 80-mile length begins at Eastbourne and currently ends near Petersfield, but an extension is planned to follow the chalk downs westward to Winchester.

Two routes leave Eastbourne, the northern climbing Willington Hill to Jevington, then above the famous Long Man of Wilmington, down to Alfriston; and the southern, a footpath only, following the cliffs past Beachy Head and over the Seven Sisters to Cuckmere Haven, then up the valley to Alfriston. Leaving the village, the Way follows the chalk escarpment over Firle Beacon in a broad sweep northwards over Ditchling Beacon to the Clayton Windmills and Pyecombe, then up again above the Devil's Dyke. The Way descends to cross the Adur valley via Bramber and Steyning, then climbs to the prominent beeches of Chanctonbury Ring. It continues, a clear track over a succession of hills, on to Amberley Mount high above the Arun. Again it crosses the valley cut through the chalk to reach the downs again above Bignor, where Roman Stane Street is signposted as it strikes across the scarp. A more wooded section follows, on Woolavington Down, and the Way drops again to cross the A286 near Cocking. On over Cocking Down it goes, past the Devil's

Jumps on to Beacon Hill, then via Harting Downs and Tower Hill, finally to descend and end near Buriton.

Such high points along the Way as Firle Beacon (713ft), Ditchling Beacon (813ft) and Beacon Hill (793ft) are fine viewpoints, but their modest height makes it clear that there is nothing rugged about the walking, which is mainly over open downland. Despite the nearness of the South Coast resorts, it is still possible to find solitude on the escarpment, except at high summer and at popular spots like Devil's Dyke. But expect to share the Way with horse-riders and cyclists, for this route is designated a bridleway. There are youth hostels at Eastbourne, Alfriston, Patcham, Trueleigh Hill and Arundel, on or near the Way, and other accommodation in the villages below the downs. Six days' walking, or more, is necessary, depending on the diversions you make in search of a night's rest.

The best short excursions are those that begin high on the downs, making use of road access and parking places. *From Beachy Head* take the up-and-down cliff walk over the Seven Sisters to Cuckmere Haven. *From near Devil's Dyke* walk west over the downs to Truleigh Hill. *From Chantry Hill*, reached by a turning off the A283, walk east to Amberley Mount. *From South Harting*, or the car park 1 mile up on the B2141, take the Way up to Beacon Hill for its views, and on perhaps to Devil's Jumps. *From Claydon* take the path up to Claydon Windmills and on to Ditchling Beacon (or park at the Beacon itself, via the road that skirts it).

South West Way

Longest, and also the least continuous, of the long-distance paths is the South West Peninsula Coast Path—515 miles in length from Minehead in Somerset down to Land's End and round to Studland by Poole Harbour. Three sections are officially open—the Dorset Coast Path of 72 miles, South Devon Coast of 93 miles, and the Cornwall Coast of 268 miles. They are open, but with breaks that occur either because the coast is deeply indented with river estuaries and developed with coast resorts, or because the coast path itself has not yet been completed.

Dorset Coast. From Studland to Lyme Regis run many miles of unspoilt, often spectacular limestone cliffs with grassy downland behind. To start the walk, you can reach Studland by ferry from Sandbanks and Bournemouth. Passing Ballard Down, the seaward end of the Purbeck Hills, the path drops to Swanage, then follows the Purbeck coast to Kimmeridge. Here the Lulworth firing ranges cause the first break; on some days it is possible to use roads across the range area, so enquire locally. The path begins again at the spectacular folded cliffs of Lulworth Cove, to follow the coast to Weymouth. At Osmington Mills an inland route is offered as an alternative, climbing over wild Dorset heathland to the Hardy Monument at 777ft, and returning to the coast beyond Abbotsbury. The coast route sets out from Weymouth over low hills to Abbotsbury, then behind the vast pebble beach of Chesil to Burton Bradstock, and thence over Golden Cap down to Lyme Regis.

South Devon Coast. This walk has great variety, with cliffs of chalk and the red sandstone of Devon, lush estuaries, sandy bays, sand bars and even a landslip. From Lyme Regis it follows the coast through Seaton and little Beer village, then Sidmouth and on to Exmouth, where a ferry crosses the estuary to Starcross. From here on, with another ferry over the Teign, the coast is punctuated by popular resorts until Torquay opens its wide bay. Beyond Brixham another ferry is needed across the Dart, and further still the path goes to seaward of the lagoon of Slapton Ley, to begin its finest stretch. High on the cliffs to Start Point, the way then turns to the glorious Salcombe inlet, rising again beyond for the National Trust's superb cliff scenery from Bolt Head to Bolt Tail. From Hope Cove on the coastline is lower and less spectacular, and the path ends at Turnchapel by Plymouth Sound.

Cornwall Coast. With rugged cliffs and headlands, great spans of uncrowded beach, and quaint villages, the 268 miles of path round the coast of Cornwall needs little description. There are some gaps and detours in the route where rights of way remain to be negotiated, where the path is too difficult to follow, or a coastal area is closed for military use, but the situation changes from year to year. There are also estuaries to cross. At Fowey,

153

Falmouth, Helford and Padstow ferries can be relied on, but at other spots—St Anthony, Gillan Harbour and Hayle, for example—it can be a case of wade, bribe or walk a long way round.

From Cremyll on the Tamar estuary, reached by ferry from Plymouth, the path sets off round Rame Head, with a turn inland to avoid a military range at Portwrinkle, to follow the cliffs of the south coast. Beyond Looe a fine stretch of cliffs extends past picturesque Polperro to Polruan, where a ferry crosses to Fowey. On past Mevagissey, further ferries are used at St Mawes (the one to St Anthony being summer-only) to reach the finest cliffs yet, around the Lizard peninsula. Little Cadgwith and Coverack villages and the serpentine cliffs of Kynance Cove are high-spots; then beyond St Michael's Mount the path ends as it enters Penzance. From Mousehole, where it starts out again, and around the sea-pounded granite headlands of Land's End, the walk is rugged and spectacular. Beyond St Ives roads will probably need to be taken into Hayle through the absence of a ferry, but from there on more good lengths of cliff scenery continue into Newquay. Around Penhale Sands again the route must detour inland to avoid a military range, and the Gannel may need wading if the summer ferry is not running. Beyond Newquay one meets sandy beaches and good cliffs again at Bedruthan Steps and Trevose Head, and a ferry at Padstow over to Rock. Around Pentire Point the coast scenery grows finer and finer, to the romantic sea-girt castle ruins of Tintagel, the narrow winding inlet of Boscastle and past the folded cliffs of Crackington Haven. Beyond Bude the cliffs rise higher and remoter still, to the county boundary at Marsland Mouth.

For the best of the Cornwall coast, explore the Land's End peninsula from Mousehole village to St Ives, the Lizard from Porthleven round to Cadgwith, or the lengths from Godrevy Point to Portreath, Mawgan Porth up to Trevose Head, or Tintagel past Boscastle to Crackington Haven.

North Devon Coast. Re-entering the county at Marsland Mouth, the cliff path immediately offers some of its finest walking, round the rugged folded rocks and reefs of the Hartland peninsula. Beyond tourist-filled Clovelly, tumbling down its hill, the path takes the Hobby Drive and on to Westward Ho!, where the estuary brings a long break in the route. It resumes at Braunton, to round Baggy Point and follow behind the glorious curve of Woolacombe Sands to Morte Point and Ilfracombe. Over Great Hangman from Ilfracombe the path reaches more fine cliff scenery by Heddon's Mouth and the Valley of Rocks to Lynmouth. Now on the seaboard edge of Exmoor, the path climbs very high over Countisbury, then detours inland to enter Somerset at County Gate, with wide views over the Brendon valley and the open moors. Dropping to cross Porlock Bay to Bossington, it climbs again to Selworthy Beacon, finally to end at the pretty Church Town end of Minehead.

There are many fine shorter cliff walks. Try those *from Speke's Mill Mouth* or *Hartland Quay* around Hartland Point, *from Hunter's Inn* and *Heddon's Mouth* to Lee Bay and Lynton, from *Porlock Weir* to tiny Culbone Church, or *from Bossington* up to Selworthy Beacon.

With both major resorts and popular seaside villages along the coast, accommodation will never be a problem, although many resorts close down out of season and can be fully booked at the height of summer. There are also many youth hostels on or near the coast: *in Dorset* at Swanage, Litton Cheney and Bridport; *in South Devon* at Beer, Exeter, Maypool near Brixham, Strete, Salcombe, Bigbury and Plymouth; *in Cornwall* at Golant, Boswinger, Falmouth, Coverack, Penzance, Land's End, Hayle, Newquay, Treyarnon Bay, Tintagel and Boscastle; and *in North Devon* at Elmscott near Hartland, Instow, Lynton and Minehead.

Cliff walking always has its dangers, of sheer drops and crumbling insecure paths. Tread carefully, especially on wet rock, and keep back from cliff edges in mist or when an offshore gale is blowing. Distances too, are deceptive; a cliff walk often involves much climbing and descending, coupled with constant minor changes of direction to skirt inlets or find easier going over a rocky headland. These factors do not show up on the map, so always make generous time allowance for them.

Offa's Dyke Path

The only long-distance route based on an archaeological rather than a topographical feature is the Offa's Dyke Path, following for much of its 168 miles the bank and ditch built by Offa, King of Mercia, in the eighth century to mark the boundary of his kingdom with Wales. The dyke remains an impressive earthwork, as much as 20ft high in places, but at two points in the journey from Chepstow on the Bristol Channel to Prestatyn on the north coast the long-distance route leaves Offa's line to follow high hill ridges.

From its marker stone by the Severn estuary Offa's Dyke Path goes to Chepstow, then up the Wye Valley, with views over Tintern Abbey, to Monmouth. Striking north-west over pastoral country, the route is well signposted past the ruins of White Castle, one of the border strongholds, to climb the eastern ridge of the Black Mountains, rising over the 2,300ft line. The moorland walk above the Vale of Ewlas ends at Hay-on-Wye, where the broad valley is crossed to take low hills via Gladestry to Kington. Beyond Kington the dyke is prominent again on Rushock Hill, and the path follows it over Herrock Hill and Furrow Hill down to Knighton. Here a 2-ton boulder commemorates the opening of the path in 1971. Across the Teme another good length of dyke is followed over Llanvair and Spode Hills, then the path runs down across lowlands near Montgomery, over Long Mountain and along the Severn bank for several miles. When the path heads northward again, it continues to trace the dyke down to the Ceiriog, then skirts the park of Chirk Castle to the Dee valley. Here all walkers with a head for heights will cross by the towpath of Telford's 120ft-high Pontcysyllte Aqueduct, with fine views down the Vale of Llangollen. The path takes the Panorama Walk above the Vale, past the ruins of Dinas Bran, beneath the limestone crags of Eglwyseg Mountain and on across the moors via ominously named World's End to Llandegla. Beyond this village the path climbs to its second ridge walk, along the Clwydian Hills, leaving the dyke entirely, finally to drop to Bodfari and the coast.

Probably no other long-distance walk offers such variety as this, from valley walking to rolling upland and bleak moorland, with a wealth of border history in its castles, abbeys and hill forts. Accommodation problems have been eased by the Offa's

156

Dyke Association and their 'where to stay' list, which gives over 100 addresses. There are also youth hostels at Severn Bridge, St Briavels (in a castle!), Capel-y-ffin, Glascwm, Clun, Llangollen and Maeshafn within a few miles of the route. With considerable climbing and descending, and moorland tops over 2,000ft, this route should be considered fairly tough walking for the best part of two weeks.

For one of the finest day walks on the Dyke, start *from Wintour's Leap* on the B4228 near Chepstow and follow it high above the Wye and Tintern to Brockweir. For some of the best of the dyke itself, follow it *from Newcastle* in the Clun valley, over Spoad and Llanvair Hills, the 6 miles to Knighton; or *at Trevor,* on the A539 Llangollen road, drop down first to the Pontcysyllte Aqueduct, then climb with the path up to the Panorama Walk and round beneath Eglwyseg.

Pembrokeshire Coast Path

The only long-distance path entirely in Wales, the 167-mile Pembrokeshire Coast Path follows the coastline of a National Park established specifically to protect this superb cliff scenery, throughout its length from Amroth to St Dogmaels. Carboniferous limestone and Old Red Sandstone cliffs alternate with wide sweeps of golden sandy beach. The coast and its offshore islands are among our finest areas for seabirds, with shearwaters, gannets, fulmars, guillemots, razorbills, puffins and kittiwakes among others. Around St David's Head, and along the north coast, the grey seals can be seen swimming and basking on the rocks, Ramsey Island being their sanctuary. Most of this can only be experienced by walkers on the coast path, access points for the carborne visitors being infrequent.

From Amroth in the south the path skirts a wide sandy bay to Saundersfoot, then to Tenby and over cliffs to Lydstep Haven. From here it detours inland to Manorbier, with its twelfth-century castle, to avoid a services training area. Following the coast again, it reaches Stackpole Head, where a much larger tank training area extends to Castlemartin, spanning some fine coastline. It is sometimes possible to follow the coast at least past St Govan's Head, but a careful check should be made before setting out, and both here and at an earlier point, Penally near Tenby, red flags will warn you if firing is in progress. Reaching the coast again at Freshwater West, the path turns the Angle peninsula to the vast Milford Haven inlet. From Pembroke the ferry can be taken over to Neyland, and beyond Milford Haven town the path comes to wild coast again round St Ann's Head and on over Marloes Sands, with Skokholm and Skomer Islands offshore, to turn Wooltack Point and head north-east past Stack Rocks to Broad Haven. From here it follows the sweep of St Brides Bay, over the shingle of Newgate beach to reach the little inlet of Solva. Rounding the St David's peninsula, the cliffs become more rugged, from St David's Head northward with tiny inlets and harbours like Porthgain and Abercastle, old slate quays, to the high cliffs of Pwll Deri. Past Strumble Head and its lighthouse, still on tall cliffs, it turns east to drop to Fishguard Harbour. Beyond Old Fishguard the path climbs to Dinas Head, then around Newport Bay and more fine cliff walking up to Cemaes Head, finally ending at the fishing village of St Dogmaels on the Teifi.

The coast path has been well prepared, by bulldozer in places, and signposted 'Coast Path' where necessary. There is strenuous walking at least on the high cliff sections, and all the comments about cliff walking on the South West Way apply equally here. The Pembrokeshire Countryside Unit by the car park at Broad Haven offers advice, lectures and a summer series of guided walks. Accommodation is not easy to find everywhere you need it, but the superb coast from St David's to Strumble Head is served by three well placed youth hostels at St David's Head, Trevine and Pwll Deri. There are also hostels at Pentlepoir behind Saundersfoot, Newport and Poppit Sands at the further end of the walk.

For highlights of the coast, it is simply a question of choosing your access point. *From Marloes* the coast can be walked from Marloes Sands round Wooltack Point to Musselwick Sands. *From Whitesand Bay*, end of the B4583, St David's Head can be explored. The fine coastline from there north-east can be joined at *Abereiddy, Abercastle* or *Aber-mawr,* and explored in either

158

direction. *From Fishguard Old Town*, or from Brynhenllan, the path can be taken out to Dinas Head.

Ridgeway Path

The 85-mile Ridgeway Path differs from the others in being something of a hybrid. The western half from Overton Hill to Streatley follows the old ridgeway track over the chalk Wessex downs and is designated a bridleway for use by horse-riders and cyclists as well as walkers; the eastern half from Goring to Ivinghoe is mainly of footpath status only, following on or above the prehistoric Icknield Way round the north escarpment of the Chilterns. Along two such ancient ways it is hardly surprising that many antiquities—hill forts and barrows, white horses and stone circles—are to be seen.

From its start on Overton Hill (on the A4) the Ridgeway has antiquities all round. Only a mile away is mysterious Silbury Hill and a footpath to the well preserved West Kennett Long Barrow, and a little further on is the giant stone circle of Avebury. Five round barrows line the Way as it starts northward as a broad track climbing the ridge of Hackpen Hill (892ft). It passes through the Iron Age ramparts of Barbury Castle, then, rather than drop down on the ancient line, it turns along the high Smeathe's Ridge to Ogbourne St George. Up on to Round Hill Downs, the track leads on again to Liddington Castle, beyond which it crosses the M4 and climbs Charlbury Hill. On it marches, past Wayland's Smithy, another chambered long barrow, to Uffington Castle on Whitehorse Hill. All these 'castles' are vast rings of earthen ramparts. Then comes Segsbury hill fort, and the old track continues its breezy upland way over Blewbury Down, finally dropping to the Thames at Streatley. Crossing the river to Goring, the path now follows a line on or near the Thames for 6 miles until, beyond Mongewell Park, it takes the line of Grim's Ditch eastwards. The old boundary ditch leads straight to Nuffield, where the path leaves it to join the Icknield Way. Following the Chiltern scarp now, it skirts Beacon Hill, climbs over Whiteleaf Hill and Coombe Hill (852ft), through Wendover and on over wooded hills to the Tring gap.

159

From here it climbs to Pitstone Hill, to end on the exposed chalk height of Ivinghoe Beacon.

It is an easy walk all the way. Accommodation can offer problems, as the Ridgeway stays high above all villages, and a series of detours will probably be needed to find a night's rest. There are youth hostels very near the route at Streatley, Lee Gate and Bradenham in the Chilterns, and Ivinghoe.

Several short excursions can sample the best of the Ridgeway walk. *From Avebury*, a fascinating base to start from, a track leads eastwards to join the Ridgeway as it climbs to Hackpen Hill and on to Barbury Castle (a Country Park). *From the B4001 road,* where the Ridgeway crosses, take it westwards to Whitehorse Hill and Wayland's Smithy, or eastwards to Segsbury Camp. *From Wendover* follow the path over Coombe Hill and Chequers Knap, or via the lane to Concord and on its waymarked route through Hale Wood to return via Wendover Forest Park. *From Beacon Hill* take the ridge walk westwards, over Steps Hill and Pitstone Hill to Aldbury.

Now to review some of the 'unofficial' long-distance walks.

Dales Way

Devised by West Riding Area of the Ramblers' Association, the

Long distance routes are not always high in the hills. The Dales Way in Langstrothdale follows the Wharfe past a stone circle in the meadows near Yockenthwaite

73-mile long Dales Way starts at Ilkley in lower Wharfedale and follows the Wharfe up into Langstrothdale, beyond which it joins the Pennine Way briefly at the head of Ribblesdale. Having crossed the north-south watershed, the Way follows the River Dee to the edge of the Yorkshire Dales National Park near Sedbergh. A cross-country route leads to the River Kent after entering the Lake District National Park, and thence to Bowness on the shores of Windermere, where the Way ends. Predominantly a valley walk, of streams, waterfalls and old villages, it crosses high moorland, reaching its highest point 1,700ft up at the Dales Way cairn on the Cam Road—so go prepared.

Coast to Coast Walk

One man's concept of a 190–mile walk across England, from St Bees in West Cumbria to Robin Hood's Bay on the east coast. But the one man is A. Wainwright, an author with such an enthusiastic following that already his Coast to Coast Walk is well used. It crosses the Lake District via Ennerdale and Honister Pass over to Grasmere, then to Patterdale and over the High Street ridge down to Shap. It runs across low hills then to Kirkby Stephen, where the high moors begin again, and over to Keld in upper Swaledale. It follows the Swale down to Richmond, a delightful old stone hilltop town, with its castle above the river. From Richmond to Ingleby Cross come 23 miles of lowland walking that Mr Wainwright is rather apologetic about, before the walk rises again to follow the north scarp of the Cleveland Hills, striking off over the North York Moors to Grosmont in the Esk valley. A final stretch crosses open moor to Hawkser, then along the high cliffs to Robin Hood's Bay. There is rugged high walking in places, but through some of the best scenery of three National Parks. If it sounds too tough, read the fascinating book instead!

Viking Way

The 50-mile section of the Viking Way open today, running over the wolds from Bigby on the borders of Lincolnshire and

South Humberside to Woodhall Spa, is only part of a much bigger concept. This length has been cleared, signposted and waymarked by Lincolnshire County Council. Eventually the Viking Way, as devised by the county council and Lincolnshire Area of the Ramblers' Association, will extend south through the county to the Leicestershire border and north to the Humber Bridge at Barton, but new paths will be needed to complete it.

Wolds Way

The 66-mile Wolds Way has been planned by East Riding Area of the Ramblers' Association, with the support of the county council. It is likely that this route will soon join the list of 'official' long-distance paths, and then new rights of way can be added to improve it. Meanwhile it is at least partly open, along existing paths. It begins on the Humber foreshore at North Ferriby, running northwards to the beginning of the Yorkshire Wolds at Melton. It turns north-west then, along the crest of the southern Wolds by Nunburnholme to Millington. From here the line runs north again past Millington Dale and Thixendale valleys. From Thixendale, in the heart of the Wolds, the Way continues to the northern escarpment and follows it, with fine views over the Vale of Pickering. It ends on the cliffs of Filey Brigg, thus linking up with the Cleveland Way to provide an even longer 160-mile route.

Essex Way

A 50-mile route through rural Essex from Epping to Dedham in the Constable Country, this Way was planned by the Essex Branch of the CPRE (Council for the Protection of Rural England). It has been considerably improved to use and open up more of the remote Essex footpaths. Accommodation can be a problem. What little there is, is hardly suitable for ramblers.

Wealdway

As an alternative to the east-west line of the North and South

162

Downs Ways, Kent ramblers have promoted the idea of a Wealdway from the Thames Estuary to the English Channel. Two sections have so far been surveyed and published—from Gravesend to Tonbridge, and Tonbridge to Uckfield.

London Countryway

Paris has for some years had a circular 'round the city' walking route, and now London has one as well. The 205-mile tour has been devised by members of the Long Distance Walkers Association, who maintain that, using the youth hostels nearby, it can be walked in a fortnight. It crosses the Kentish weald, follows the North Downs, reaches the Thames via Windsor Park and follows the river for a while before setting off through the Chilterns and rural Hertfordshire to Epping Forest and back to the Thames estuary again via Essex paths.

Cotswold Way

This 100-mile route follows the steep western escarpment of the Cotswolds in its journey from mellow old Chipping Campden in Gloucestershire to Bath in Avon. At points it offers fine views over Evesham and Severn Vales, and leads through such delightful stone villages as Broadway, Stanton and Stanway, Winchcombe, Birdlip and Painswick. It also runs by Seven Springs, argued by some to be the source of the Thames. It was devised by the Gloucestershire and Avon Areas of the Ramblers' Association in conjunction with the respective county councils, and is the first long-distance route to be waymarked throughout with the Countryside Commission's yellow and blue arrows. The organisers describe it as a 7 to 9–day walk for 'any reasonably active person'.

North Bucks Way

A pleasant 30-mile route from Chequers Knap on the Chiltern escarpment north over the Vale of Aylesbury to Wolverton, this route was planned, improved and waymarked by local Ramblers'

Association members with county council support, as an introduction to the rather neglected footpaths of the Vale. A good 2-day walk, it has a convenient half-way hostelry for an overnight stop.

Oxfordshire Way

A route of over 60 miles across the county, devised by the Oxfordshire Branch of the CPRE, it begins at Henley-on-Thames, crosses the Chiltern Hills and the lowlands north of Oxford, and follows the Evenlode valley, eventually to turn off to Bourton-on-the-Water in the Cotswolds.

Two Moors Way

The original exciting concept of a long-distance bridleway linking the Devon coasts across Dartmoor and Exmoor could not be realised, owing to opposition from landowners. The Two Moors Way open today is a footpath route from Ivybridge to Lynmouth, using existing rights of way entirely, except for a few diversions agreed for local convenience. It was surveyed and mapped by Devon Area of the Ramblers' Association, with the backing of Devon County Council. From Ivybridge the Way climbs immediately on to the barren southern heights of Dartmoor, crossing to Holne village and via the deep wooded valley of Holne Chase on to the moor again by Widecombe. The route pulls up over Hamel Down, then briefly follows the old (and now waymarked) Mariners Way to Chagford and along the Teign to Drewsteignton. From here, leaving Dartmoor National Park, it takes to muddy fieldpaths and lanes through mid-Devon via Morchard Bishop and Hawkridge, then follows the beautiful wooded valley of the Barle to Withypool. Beyond, the Way climbs on to open Exmoor heights to Exe Head, and follows the Hoar Oak Water down to Lynmouth. The whole 103-mile walk, with diversions in search of accommodation, will need about 10 days, with high moorland, fine river valleys and pretty cob and thatch villages on the way. There is plenty of variety but hard walking.

11 Getting More from a Country Walk

A walk in the country can bring you satisfaction besides the enjoyment of landscape and physical well-being. You may already have some particular interest that a country walk will give opportunities to develop—photography, geology, bird-watching, or collecting wild flowers or fossils. Even without such a previous inclination, you can find a new interest arising naturally from a day in the country. Walking quietly through the woods and fields you will spot more birds, flowers, butterflies, insects and fungi in a ten mile round than you would see in twenty times that distance along roads.

Bear this in mind when you pack for a day's walk. If you are a photographer, take your camera even if it normally only comes out on holiday or visits to stately homes. If you have any interest in wild life, pack a polythene bag or two, or a yoghurt carton for bringing specimens home; or carry a book on identifying birds, butterflies or wildflowers; or a scrapbook for pressing flowers and leaves. If you bring binoculars for bird-watching or observing animals, use them also for picking out landmarks to follow your route by, or for spotting a stile on the far side of a wide field. Paper and pencil will be useful for sketching a scene that interests you—a type of barn or gable end, a strange fungus or butterfly —anything you want to remember and identify later. Even without a specific interest, a spare bag or picnic box comes in useful for blackberries, mushrooms or nuts—most of us are 'collectors' in that sense!

Wild Life

An interest in wild life will enliven a country walk even on a 'misty moisty morning', when the distant view disappears, and the nearby is shrouded in greyness. It will also make a familiar path continuously fascinating throughout the year as its wild life changes with the seasons. Notice how winter brings to light the

165

stark beauty of the shape of trees, their contrasting outlines clear against the sky. If you enjoy not just the sight of a wildflower but the satisfaction of being able to name it, remember that to identify and illustrate *all* the varieties of even common species, a handbook needs to be quite big. If it is too heavy or bulky to carry around, it is better to make notes and sketches on the spot of any specimen you suspect may be rare rather than risk picking something irreplaceable. Even common wild flowers should be picked with care not to damage the plant. For non-specialists the pocket-sized 'Observer's' series will be sufficient to identify the types most frequently met with.

The fauna of the countryside are naturally less predictable in their appearances than its flora, but even the most unobservant rambler will catch on every walk the song and often the sight of many birds that do not frequent towns, and sooner or later the less common wild animals, such as weasels, stoats, foxes and hares will cross his path, as well as the more familiar squirrels and rabbits. There may be otters and voles by river banks; lizards, slow-worms and grass snakes; a pool alive with young frogs; perhaps even deer. Motorists may think deer are only to be seen behind park fences or in the remotest parts of the Highlands and Exmoor. While this is true of red deer, regular walkers know that roe or fallow deer may cross their path in the most unexpected places—on the edge of a Surrey field, for example, no more than 20 miles from London. But *never* within sight or sound of a road!

Geology

Geology is a science that the countrygoer learns with his feet. The underlying rocks explain the ups and downs of a day's walk, and why you are slithering on loose scree at one point on your path and ankle-deep in bog at another. But if you turn to a basic textbook of geology for the answers you may find yourself rather out of your depth in the Lower Palaeozoic. It is better to start with reading up the geology of your particular area than try to understand all the general principles first. A local geological handbook or even a chapter in the local guidebook may be enough to explain the particular hill contours, drainage patterns, types of soil and farming you will see. The important thing is to notice the variations, such as the different types of scenery produced by the chalk of the North Downs, with its bold escarpment rising to Box Hill, and the greensand ridge of Leith Hill and its neighbours only half a dozen miles to the south. If you visit certain areas for their distinctive or spectacular landscape, it is their geological structure that has attracted you there, whether you know it or not: the granite tors of Dartmoor weathered into fantastic shapes, the curious limestone 'pavement' above Malham Cove, Cheddar Gorge cut through the limestone of the Mendips, the chalk cliffs of the Seven Sisters, or the jagged outline of the Cuillins carved in gabbro. You may become interested in the subject by picking up individual stones that catch your eye—or stub your toe. Observing the differences and learning what type of rock they come from, you come to understand something of the underlying structure of the land you walk on. A collection of stones can make a beautiful and interesting display. Keep them grouped as you find them, and, if possible, label them.

The same goes for collecting fossils, which are of major interest in certain areas. In parts of the Craven district of Yorkshire, for instance, the drystone walls are almost built of fossils, and the beaches at Lyme Regis and Whitby are a happy fossil-hunting ground, particularly for the most beautiful ammonites, which abound in the Blue Lias there. If you are going to walk in a region known to contain many fossils, it is worth taking a hammer. (Failing a proper geological hammer, a light glazier's hammer will do.) Otherwise your most spectacular find may remain immovably stuck in an enormous boulder, or you may find yourself carrying a pack full of large rocks that get heavier and more knobbly every mile.

Landscape History

Landscape history has only been systematically studied relatively recently. W. G. Hoskins's *The Making of the English Landscape* was the first general study of this subject. He and others have since developed it further; there have been some excellent local studies, too, and a county series that already covers a dozen counties. It is worth looking to see if the area you walk in is covered.

The history of the landscape brings together themes from many different fields of study to interpret what we see around us now. Geology, climate, early settlement, land-ownership customs, types of farming, growth of markets, routes of communication, enclosure, rural industries and many other factors all come into the picture of our countryside as we see it today. You will be walking through the countryside at a leisurely enough pace to notice the detail that builds up the picture. The very footpath you are walking on is part of the history of the landscape, and one day's walk may take you through stages of its development covering several centuries. Once you have absorbed some of the ideas, you may be able to make an intelligent guess as to why this narrow track zigzags round odd-shaped fields, while another makes straight across the countryside wide enough for a whole herd of cattle (they may have made it); which hedge bank or ditch was a boundary back in the days of *Domesday Book* and which date from eighteenth-century enclosure. You might stop to count the different species of shrub in a hedge; it has been estimated that for every different shrub species in a 30yd length of hedge we can reckon 100 years of life. In any case it is a fascinating subject and a little preliminary knowledge will open your eyes to much you would otherwise miss. Hoskins quotes Constable for his theme: 'We see nothing till we truly understand it.'

Nature Trails

Whether you intended to or not, you may occasionally find yourself following the route of a Nature Trail, for trails have proliferated since National Nature Week in 1963, when the idea first caught on in this country. A Nature Trail is a waymarked walk designed to draw the visitor's attention to aspects of the wild life visible along it. It does this sometimes by means of descriptive panels along the route, but more often you will find only numbered posts, and the information about what is to be seen at each point is provided in a leaflet. This will always

The Forestry Commission's Nine Becks Walk begins at Ennerdale
Water in the Lake District, leading through Forest and open fell.
This bridge over Deep Gill was financed by the Ramblers'
Association and the county council

include the flowers, trees and the full range of its botanical life,
together with its likely animal and bird population; but some
trails have an additional point of interest, such as the old iron-
industry workings at Horam Quiet Corner, Sussex, or the chalk/
flint quarries on Coulsdon Downs. The guide leaflets, costing
usually only a few pence, are available locally, sometimes at the
starting point of the trail, particularly if it starts in a car park;
otherwise they are to be found at information centres, refreshment huts, Forestry Commission offices, local shops and garages,
council offices, National Trust houses and so on, depending on
what body is responsible for the trail. Most trails are very short,
from $\frac{1}{2}$ to 5 miles, though the Isle of Wight goes in for longish
ones. If you like the idea of having an expert in your pocket, as
it were, to point out the Great Hairy Woodrush you would have
failed to notice and the ecological significance you would have

A family takes the West Wycombe Farm Trail in the Chilterns. West Wycombe church and village are in the background

failed to recognise, it would be worth finding out what trails are open in your walking area and where you can obtain guide leaflets in advance. The British Tourist Authority publishes a list with location, brief details of what is to be seen and the address for the leaflet—*Nature Trails in Britain.*

Forest Trails are a specialised form of Nature Trails in woodland, usually with an emphasis on the management of woodland as well as its natural ecology. Many are provided by the Forestry Commission, which has opened half a dozen in the Forest of Dean alone.

Farm Trails are a rarer species. The Countryside Commission arranged an experimental series of fifteen in 1976 as part of a scheme to increase public understanding of farming life. The farmers taking part allow visitors to walk around their fields following trails, most of which of course are not public rights of

170

way, to study their crops, stock and farming methods. Many of these farms also hold Open Days and similar activities. Some other farms also operate trails on their own initiative or in cooperation with local organisations, but there does not appear to be any central register and probably not many of them are permanently open. The Countryside Commission hopes to extend the scheme, following the success of this first venture. A leaflet on the trails so far established can be obtained from the Countryside Commission, or from the Association of Agriculture, Victoria Chambers, 16–20 Strutton Ground, London, SW1.

Walking with Children

Children can enjoy a walk in the countryside from a very early age. A 4-year-old may join in a family walk of 8 miles, probably travelling half of this on his father's shoulders. Obviously children's capacity, stamina and inclination vary widely, but as a very rough guide you may reckon that a child can walk at least as many miles as he has years of age, *provided* he is taken out for walks frequently *and* that he enjoys it. He enjoys it in a different way from his parents. His eyes will not be on the distant landscape, they will be on the minutiae of the countryside around him. The regular striding for an hour or two at a time which is an adult walker's pattern is not natural for him. He will want to stop whenever he sees something of interest, to look down into a burrow, pick a strange fungus, explore a cleft in the hillside above him, talk to a friendly horse, or roll down a steep grassy slope. A boring steady trudge will tire him more than some unnecessary scampering or a strenuous but exciting climb. More than anything else it is his quick eye for detail that will make a country walk interesting to him, and to others. One really observant and scientifically minded child will turn a whole family into naturalists or geologists.

If some of the children start saying they 'don't like walking', treat a day out as an expedition with a particular objective—a lake to fish in, a stream to dam, a cave to play cavemen in, the spoil heaps of a disused mine to hunt for treasure in. Arrange a long stop here, preferably at lunchtime, with enough time to make it seem the main point of the expedition. They may well enjoy the walk there and back unconsciously just because they are not expected to enjoy it for its own sake. If animals and birds are disappointingly absent on a naturalists' expedition, set them looking for their tracks and trails— a whole subject in itself—and such other traces as droppings and debris (split nutshells left by squirrels, for instance). Turn over an old log or boulder to watch the creepy crawlies that emerge. (But be sure to put it back.) You need not take balls or toys; it is better for a child to make his own fun from what he finds around him when you stop, even if it is only throwing stones into a stream.

Collecting. All children are born collectors. They start off with the magpie habit—the pockets of their wind-cheaters will be stuffed with a most miscellaneous haul of stones, cartridge cases, berries, fungi, conkers, acorns, leaf skeletons, even a dead mouse or mole. Have plenty of bags available for 'finds' that need careful packing, and keep a corner or a shelf to display their treasures at home. Do not try to impose an adult's division into worthwhile and worthless, but encourage them to identify their finds where appropriate. Local museums can be very useful here— they often display the types of fossils, rocks and early artefacts found locally, and sometimes also the distinctive local flora and fauna, and a child will feel very proud to see the 'twin' of his fossil important enough to be displayed in a glass case. Large specialised museums such as the Geological Museum at South Kensington will have a library staffed by specialists who will identify a whole pocketful of assorted rocks or fossils without batting an eyelid. As they begin to specialise and follow one interest in greater depth, back it up with handbooks, scrapbooks or collecting jars. One child's interest can enrich a whole family's appreciation of the country.

Farms. Teach children to respect the farming life of the countryside. If you pass by cowsheds at milking time, or chance on a combine harvester at work, or a flock of sheep being rounded up by sheepdogs, take time to watch. Children will understand more clearly that the fields they walk through, even the rough pasture they picnic on, are someone's property and livelihood. Where they come to play, others come to work, and farming is as much a part of the countryside as rabbits and skylarks, black-berries and acorns.

Maps. An adult studies the map before setting out and relates the landscape he sees to the mental picture the map has supplied. With a child it is better, at first, to work the other way round. He will not get much idea by looking at a map in advance, but let him sprawl on the floor with the map afterwards, point out the route you followed and one or two salient features, and he will soon be triumphantly pinpointing the stream you crossed, the hill you climbed, the wood where you found nuts. He will probably be ten or more before he is confident enough to pick out on the ground the path he can find easily enough on the map.

Geography. If a child has already learned some of the elements of geography and geology at school, he should be able with a little help to relate them to what he sees in the country—but he may not think of doing so unless you prompt him to do so. Until someone points out the abandoned river terraces or the glaciated U-shaped valley, what he has learned in the classroom may remain shut away with his books. Once a child's eyes are opened in this way, he begins to understand the relationship between theory and practical examples. It should become a two-way process. As his understanding of the land forms he sees is deepened, so he absorbs the theoretical knowledge he has been taught at school, and he learns to apply it to interpret the countryside he walks through.

Useful Books

GENERAL

Margery, I. D. *Roman Ways in the Weald* (1948)

Smith, Brian. *The Cotswolds* (1976)

GEOLOGY

Geological Survey of Great Britain. Regional handbooks (HMSO)
A long series of pamphlets, each describing in detail the geology of a small area, eg *The Coast between Tintagel and Bude, Around Wells and Cheddar.* Full list from HMSO.

Geology Explained series (David & Charles)
Regional studies on the understanding of landscape, its origin and evolution. No previous knowledge of geology is assumed. Regions covered so far: *Dartmoor and the Tamar Valley, Forest of Dean and Wye Valley, North Wales, Peak District, Severn Vale and Cotswolds, South and East Devon, South Wales.*

LANDSCAPE HISTORY

Baker, A. and Harley, J. B. *Man Made the Land* (David & Charles)
A reinterpretation of the historical geography of England, tracing the development of the English landscape.

Hoskins, W. G. *English Landscapes* (BBC)
The Making of the English Landscape: how to read the man-made scenery of England (Hodder; and Penguin)

Hoskins, W. G. and Millward, R. (eds). *The Making of the English Landscape* series (Hodder)
Introductory volume by W. G. Hoskins; new ed in preparation, 1977. Counties covered so far: Cambridgeshire, Cornwall, Dorset, Gloucestershire, Lancashire, Leicestershire, Northamptonshire, Northumberland, Oxfordshire, Shropshire, South Wales, Staffordshire, Suffolk, Sussex, West Riding of Yorkshire. Volumes on Hertfordshire, Norfolk and North Riding of Yorkshire in preparation, 1977–8.

Lively, Penelope. *The Presence of the Past: an introduction to landscape history* (Collins)

WILD LIFE

Allen, Grace and Denslow, Joan. (eds). *Clue Books* (OUP)
Invaluable for children, helping them to compare things of the same kind, spot the differences and arrange their findings. They

divide specimens by visible characteristics, each 'clue' leading to further subdivisions on a later page until the specimen is identified. Illustrated with very clear, carefully drawn diagrams. Titles: *Birds, Bones, Flowerless Plants, Flowers, Freshwater Animals, Insects, Seashore Animals, Trees.*

Collins Field and Pocket Guides (Collins)

An excellent series, well known to the naturalist, but beware—the *Pocket Guides* are no smaller than the *Field Guides*, and are far too large and heavy for any normal pocket, though worth a place in a pack. Identification is made easy by the system of 'keys', eg trees are divided by leaf shape and bark type, with special keys to various species such as conifers. Comprehensive, well illustrated and practical, and intended for field work. Titles include *Animal Tracks and Signs, Bird Watching, Birds of Britain and Europe, Butterflies of Britain and Europe, Freshwater Fishes of Britain and Europe. A Guide to the British Landscape, Mammals of Britain and Europe, Mushrooms and Toadstools, Nests and Eggs, Rocks and Minerals of the World, Trees of Britain and Northern Europe, Wild Flowers.* (*A Guide to the British Landscape* covers geology in some detail, with shorter sections on selected wild life, agriculture, prehistory, buildings etc.)

New Naturalist series (Collins)

A well known series, and reference books rather than field handbooks. Besides numerous naturalists' titles, they include some basic books on geology and the landscape, such as *Britain's Structure and Scenery* (also Fontana paperback), *The English Coast and Coast of Wales, Man and the Land, A Natural History of Man in Britain.*

Observer's Books (Warne)

Inexpensive handbooks, small enough to fit into an anorak pocket, yet containing enough for beginners and non-specialists. Ninety titles in series. Useful titles for walkers include *Birds, Birds' Eggs, Butterflies, Common Insects and Spiders, Freshwater Fishes, Grasses, Larger Moths, Pond Life, Sea and Seashore, Sedges and Rushes, Trees, Wild Animals of the British Isles, Wild Flowers.*

Regional Naturalist series (David & Charles)

Not field guides, but useful in showing what to look out for in specific areas. Regions covered so far: Central Southern England, Devon and Cornwall, Isle of Man, Lakeland, London, South East England, Wales.

Appendix 1 Useful Organisations

The BRITISH TOURIST AUTHORITY, the ENGLISH TOURIST BOARD, the SCOTTISH TOURIST BOARD and the WALES TOURIST BOARD exist to promote tourism in their respective territories and to provide information for tourists.

British Tourist Authority, 64 St James Street, London SW1 (Tel: 01-629 9191).

English Tourist Board, 4 Grosvenor Gardens, London SW1W 0DU (Tel: 01-730 3400).

Scottish Tourist Board, Croythorn House, 23 Ravelston Terrace, Edinburgh 4 (Tel: 031-332 2433).

Wales Tourist Board, Welcome House, Llandaff, Cardiff (Tel: Cardiff 567701).

The COMMONS, OPEN SPACES AND FOOTPATHS PRESERVATION SOCIETY, the Commons Society for short, aims to promote knowledge of the law, so that paths and commons may be preserved for the public benefit. Members receive a journal twice a year, and the Society's other publications. Best known is their 50-page *Practical Guide to the Law of Footpaths*.

The Commons Society, 166 Shaftesbury Avenue, London WC2H 8JH (Tel: 01-836 7220).

The COUNCIL FOR THE PROTECTION OF RURAL ENGLAND, and its sister council for Wales, act to improve, protect and preserve the rural scenery and amenities of the countryside, its towns and villages.

Council for the Protection of Rural England, 4 Hobart Place, London SW1W 0HY (Tel: 01-235 9481).

Council for the Protection of Rural Wales, Meifod, Montgomery, Powys SY22 6DA (Tel: Meifod 383).

The COUNTRYSIDE COMMISSION is the government agency charged with the protection of the countryside. It is responsible for the designation and general overseeing of National Parks and Areas of Outstanding Natural Beauty. It issues many publications, including free literature on National Parks and official long-distance paths.

Countryside Commission, John Dower House, Crescent Place, Cheltenham, Glos. GL50 3RA (Tel: Cheltenham 21381).

National Parks (Some information centres are open only on certain days, or at certain times of year).

Brecon Beacons: National Park Office, 6 Glamorgan Street, Brecon, Powys. Information centres at Abergavenny, Libanus and Llandovery.

176

Dartmoor: National Park Office, County Hall, Exeter. Three mobile information centres.

Exmoor: National Park Office, Exmoor House, Dulverton, Somerset. Information centres at Combe Martin, Lynmouth and Minehead.

Lake District: National Park Office, County Hall, Kendal, Cumbria. National Park Centre at Brockhole, on A591 between Ambleside and Windermere. Information centres at Ambleside, Bowness, Coniston, Glenridding, Hawkshead, Keswick, Seatoller and Waterhead at the head of Windermere.

Northumberland: National Park Office, Bede House, All Saints Centre, Newcastle upon Tyne. Information centres at Byrness, Ingram, Once Brewed and Rothbury.

North York Moors: National Park Office, The Old Vicarage, Bondgate, Helmsley, North Yorkshire. National Park Centre at Danby Lodge, Danby, Castleton. Information centres at Pickering and Sutton Bank.

Peak District: National Park Office, Aldern House, Baslow Road, Bakewell, Derbyshire. Information centres at Bakewell, Buxton, Castleton, Dovestones, Edale, Goyt Valley and Hartington.

Pembrokeshire Coast: National Park Office, County Offices, Haverfordwest, Dyfed. Information centres at Broad Haven, Fishguard, Haverfordwest, Kilgetty, Pembroke, St David's and Tenby.

Snowdonia: National Park Office, The Old School House, Maentwrog, Gwynedd. Information centres at Aberdyfi, Bala, Blaenau' Ffestiniog, Conway, Dolgellau, Harlech, Llanberis and Llanrwst.

Yorkshire Dales: National Park Office, 'Colvend', Hebden Road, Grassington, Skipton, North Yorkshire. Information centres at Aysgarth Falls, Clapham, Hawes, Malham, Sedbergh and Settle.

The FORESTRY COMMISSION manages the national forestry enterprise and provides grants and advice to private forestry. It allows free access to walkers in most of its plantations. Guides to many of the forest areas are published by HMSO.

Forestry Commission, 231 Corstorphine Road, Edinburgh EH12 7AT (Tel: 031-334 0303).

The HOLIDAY FELLOWSHIP and COUNTRY-WIDE HOLIDAYS ASSOCIATION (HF and CHA for short) both run holiday centres of guesthouse type in many of the best landscape areas of Britain. Their holiday parties have an emphasis on walking, in several grades.

The Holiday Fellowship, 142 Great North Way, Hendon, London NW4 1EG (Tel: 01-203 3381).

Country-Wide Holidays Association, Birch Hays, Cromwell Range, Manchester M14 6HU.

The NATURE CONSERVANCY COUNCIL is the government body concerned with nature conservation. The Council declares and maintains National Nature Reserves and provides advice and information about nature conservation.

Nature Conservancy Council, 19/20 Belgrave Square, London SW1X 8PY (Tel: 01-235 3241).

The NATIONAL TRUST for places of historic interest or natural beauty is an independent body, with rights and duties laid down by Parliament. It owns over 350,000 acres and many historic buildings, permanently preserved for the nation. Much of the open country owned by the Trust is open to the public free of charge. Members obtain free entry to Trust properties.

National Trust, 42 Queen Anne's Gate, London SW1 (Tel: 01-930 0211).

The ORDNANCE SURVEY is the government agency responsible for the survey and mapping of Great Britain. Its best known maps for walkers are those at 1:25,000 and 1:50,000 scale.

Ordnance Survey, Romsey Road, Maybush, Southampton SO9 4DH (Tel: Southampton 775555).

The RAMBLERS' ASSOCIATION is the national organisation concerned with the protection and promotion of rights of way and access to open country. It also takes an active interest in preserving the countryside. The Association has 30,000 individual members, local branches and many affiliated rambling clubs throughout the country. Publications include useful Fact Sheets on local path guides and an annual bed-and-breakfast guide.

Ramblers' Association, Crawford Mews, York Street, London W1H 1PT. (Tel: 01-262 1477/8).

The SOCIETY FOR THE PROMOTION OF NATURE CONSERVATION coordinates the work of, and provides information about, the County Trusts for Nature Conservation.

Society for the Promotion of Nature Conservation, The Green, Nettleham, Lincoln.

The YOUTH HOSTELS ASSOCIATION has a chain of 250 youth hostels throughout England and Wales. Despite the name, the hostels are open to members of all ages. The Association has many local groups and an annual programme of Adventure Holidays for ages 11 up.

Youth Hostels Association, Trevelyan House, St Albans, Herts, AL1 2DY. (Tel: St Albans 55215). Also Regional Offices and YHA shops in London, Birkenhead, Birmingham, Cardiff, Colchester, Durham, Manchester, Matlock, Plymouth and Windermere.

The SCOTTISH YOUTH HOSTELS ASSOCIATION has a chain of 81 youth hostels throughout Scotland. Conditions of membership as above.

Scottish Youth Hostels Association, 7 Glebe Crescent, Stirling FK8 2JA (Tel: Stirling 2821).

Appendix 2   Maps and Guides

Many of the guides listed in this section are not widely available except in local bookshops, and for this reason we have provided publishers' addresses where appropriate. Some names appear frequently and for convenience we give the addresses below:

BBC Publications, 35 Marylebone High Street, London W1M 4AA.
Dalesman Publishing Co., Clapham via Lancaster.
Footpath Publications, Adstock Cottage, Adstock, Buckingham.
Gerrard Publications, 26 Manor Road, Harrow, Middlesex.
RA (Ramblers' Association), Crawford Mews, York Street, London W1H 1PT.
Shire Publications, Cromwell House, Church Street, Princes Risborough, Bucks.
Spurbooks, 6 Parade Court, Bourne End, Bucks.
Thornhill Press, 7 Russell Street, Gloucester.
Westmorland Gazette, 22 Stricklandgate, Kendal, Cumbria.

The order in which the walks and ways are listed follows that of Chapters 8–10, in general starting in the north and running clockwise round the country.

HILL COUNTRY

LAKE DISTRICT
Maps
OS 1:50,000 sheets 85, 89, 90, 96
  One-inch tourist map—The Lake District
  1:25,000 Outdoor Leisure Maps—SE (Windermere and Kendal), NE (Ullswater and Haweswater), NW (Ennerdale and Derwent) and SW (Wastwater and Coniston).
Guides
Lake District National Park Guide (HMSO)
The Lakeland Peaks—W. A. Poucher (Constable)
A Pictorial Guide to the Lakeland Fells—A. Wainwright (*Westmorland Gazette*)
  1 *The Eastern Fells*
  2 *The Far Eastern Fells*
  3 *The Central Fells*

4 *The Southern Fells*
5 *The Northern Fells*
6 *The North Western Fells*
7 *The Western Fells*
The Outlying Fells of Lakeland
Walking in Northern Lakeland—Peter Lewis and Brian Porter (Dalesman)
Walking in Central Lakeland—Brian and Joy Greenwood (Dalesman)
Walking in Southern Lakeland—Brian and Joy Greenwood (Dalesman)

CHEVIOTS
Maps
OS 1:50,000 sheets 74, 80, 81, 86
Guides
Ramblers Cheviot (Harold Hill & Son, Killingsworth Place, Gallowgate, Newcastle NE1 4SL)

NORTH PENNINES
Maps
OS 1:50,000 sheets 86, 87, 91, 92

NORTH YORK MOORS
OS 1:50,000 sheets 93, 94, 100, 101
    One-inch tourist map—North York Moors
Guides
North York Moors National Park Guide (HMSO)
North York Moors Walks for Motorists—*North and East, West and South* (Gerrard)
North Yorkshire Forests—Forestry Commission (HMSO)
Walking on the North York Moors (Dalesman)

YORKSHIRE DALES
Maps
OS 1:50,000 sheets 91, 92, 97, 98, 99, 103, 104
    1:25,000 Outdoor Leisure Maps—Malham & Upper Wharfedale, The Three Peaks
Guides
Yorkshire Dales National Park Guide (HMSO)
Yorkshire Dales Walks for Motorists (Gerrard)
Walking in the Craven Dales—Speakman (Dalesman)
Walks in Limestone Country—A. Wainwright (*Westmorland Gazette*)
The Peak and Pennines—W. A. Poucher (Constable)

DARK PEAK

Maps

OS 1:50,000 sheet 110

    One-inch Tourist map—The Peak District

    1:25,000 Outdoor Leisure Map—The Dark Peak

Guides

The Peak and Pennines—W. A. Poucher (Constable)

Walks around Edale (from the Peak Park Planning Board)

Walks around Longdendale (from the Peak Park Planning Board)

DARTMOOR

Maps

OS 1:50,000 sheets 191, 201, 202

    One-inch tourist map—Dartmoor

Guides

Dartmoor National Park Guide (HMSO)

Crossing's Guide to Dartmoor (David & Charles)

Waymarked Walks on Dartmoor (County Tourist Office, Trinity Court, Southernhay East, Exeter EX1 1PD)

EXMOOR

Maps

OS 1:50,000 sheets 180, 181

    One-inch tourist map—Exmoor

Guides

Exmoor National Park Guide (HMSO)

Exmoor Walks; Exmoor Coastal Walks—Tim Abbott (Cider Press, Hillside, Martlett Road, Minehead, Somerset)

Waymarked Walks in Exmoor National Park (from Exmoor House, Dulverton, Somerset)

    1 Dunster, Minehead, Brendon, Luxborough, Roadwater

    2 Porlock, Oare, Dunkery, Malmsmead, Exford, Simonsbath

    3 Dulverton, Winsford Hill, Tarr Steps, Anstey Common, Haddeo Valley

QUANTOCKS

Map

OS 1:50,000 sheet 181

BODMIN MOOR

Maps

OS 1:50,000 sheets 200, 201

BRECON BEACONS AND BLACK MOUNTAINS

Maps

OS 1:50,000 sheets 159, 160, 161

    1:25,000 Outdoor Leisure Maps—Eastern (Abergavenny and

the Black Mountains), Central (Brecon and the Beacons), Western (Llandeilo and the Black Mountain)

Guides
Brecon Beacons National Park Guide (HMSO)
Exploring the Waterfall Country—Chris Barber (T. Pridgeon, Marks Farmhouse, Llangrove, Ross-on-Wye)
Walks in the Brecon Beacons—Chris Barber

SHROPSHIRE HILLS
Maps
OS 1:50,000 sheets 126, 137
Guide
Church Stretton Rambles—Robert Smart (from the author at Brackendale, Longhills Road, Church Stretton, Shropshire)

CENTRAL WALES
Maps
OS 1:50,000 sheets 135, 136, 146, 147
Guides
Elenith—Timothy Porter (YHA, 35 Park Place, Cardiff)
From Offa's Dyke to the Sea—Carl Ehrenzeller (St Christopher's, Llandrindod Wells, Powys)
Rambles round Radnorshire—Carl Ehrenzeller

SNOWDONIA
Maps
OS 1:50,000 sheets 115, 116, 124, 125, 135
    1:25,000 Outdoor Leisure Maps in preparation
Guides
Snowdonia National Park Guide (HMSO)
Snowdonia Forest Park Guide—Forestry Commission (HMSO)
Hill Walking in Snowdonia—E. G. Rowland (Cicerone Press, 16 Briarsfield Road, Worsley, Manchester)
The Welsh Peaks—W. A. Poucher (Constable)

FOREST OF BOWLAND AND PENDLE HILL
Maps
OS 1:50,000 sheets 97, 98, 102, 103
Guides
Bowland and Pendle Hill—W. R. Mitchell (Dalesman)
Pendleside and Brontë Country Walks for Motorists (Gerrard)

YORKSHIRE WOLDS
Maps
OS 1:50,000 sheets, 101, 106
Guide
Walking in East Yorkshire—Geoff Eastwood (from the author, 60 Front Street, Lockington, Driffield, Humberside)

WHITE PEAK
Maps
OS 1:50,000 sheets 118, 119
One-inch tourist map—The Peak District
Guides
Peak National Park Guide (HMSO)
Peak District Walks for Motorists (Gerrard)
Walks around Dovedale, Bakewell, Eyam and Hathersage (Peak Park Planning Board)
Peak District Walks—John N. Merrill (Dalesman)
1 *Short Walks*
2 *Long Walks*

CHILTERN HILLS
Maps
OS 1:50,000 sheets 165, 175
Chiltern Society footpath maps: Chartridge, Marlow, Penn, Wendover, Wycombe NW (Shire Publications)
Guides
Chiltern Round Walks—Vera Burden (Spurbooks)
Discovering Walks in Buckinghamshire—Ronald Pilgrim (Shire Publications)

SURREY HILLS
Maps
OS 1:50,000 sheets 186, 187
Guide
Walks in the Surrey Hills—Janet Spayne and Audrey Krynski (Spurbooks)

SOUTH DOWNS
Maps
OS 1:50,000 sheets 197, 198, 199
1:25,000 Outdoor Leisure Map—Brighton and Sussex Vale
Guides
Discovering Walks in West Sussex—T. W. Hendrick (Shire Publications)

On Foot in East Sussex (Eastbourne Rambling Club, 28 Kinfauns Avenue, Eastbourne)

South Sussex Walks—Lord Teviot and M. B. Quinion (BBC Publications)

ISLE OF WIGHT
Map
OS 1:50,000 sheet 196
Guides
Guides to several trails using rights of way can be obtained from the County Surveyor, Isle of Wight CC, Newport IOW.

NEW FOREST
Maps
OS 1:50,000 sheets 195, 196
  One-inch tourist map—The New Forest
Guides
Explore the New Forest—Forestry Commission (HMSO)
Discovering Walks in the New Forest—Derrick Knowlton (Shire Publications)
New Forest Walks—Anne-Marie Edwards (BBC Publications)
Walks in the New Forest—W. Wenban Smith (Spurbooks)

WESSEX DOWNS
Maps
OS 1:50,000 sheets 173, 174, 184
Guides
Nine Downland Walks South of Swindon—RA Wiltshire Area (A. Toomer, 24, Calsbrook Terrace, Chiseldon, Swindon)
Walks in Berkshire—Vera Burden (Spurbooks)

PURBECK AND DORSET COAST
Maps
OS 1:50,000 sheets 193, 194, 195
  1:25,000 Outdoor Leisure Map in preparation
Guide
Walks in Dorset—G. H. Osborn (Spurbooks)

MENDIPS
Maps
OS 1:50,000 sheets 182, 183

COTSWOLDS
Maps
OS 1:50,000 sheets 150, 151, 162, 163, 173

Ramblers' Maps of the Cotswolds—RA Gloucestershire Area
(Miss M. A. Brooks, 85 Broadoak Way, Cheltenham GL51
5LL)
1 Birdlip
2 Cleeve Hill
Guides
Cotswold Rambles—Drinkwater and Hargreaves (Thornhill Press)
Cotswold Walks for Motorists—P. A. Price (Gerrard)
1 *Northern*
2 *Southern*

WYE VALLEY AND FOREST OF DEAN
Maps
OS 1:50,000 sheet 162
1:25,000 Outdoor Leisure Map in preparation
Guides
Dean and Wye Valley Forest Park—Forestry Commission (HMSO)
Waymarked Paths in the Forest of Dean—(from Miss D. Knight,
Cotswold House, Fauconberg Road, Cheltenham)
Waymarked Paths in Highmeadow Woods—(from Miss D. Knight)

GOWER PENINSULA
Map
OS 1:50,000 sheet 159

ARNSIDE AND SILVERDALE
Map
OS 1:50,000 sheet 97

LONG-DISTANCE ROUTES

PENNINE WAY
Maps
OS 1:50,000 sheets 74, 80, 86, 91, 92, 98, 103, 109, 110
Guides
Pennine Way—Tom Stephenson (HMSO)
Pennine Way—Tom Stephenson (Ramblers' Association)
Pennine Way Companion—A. Wainwright (*Westmorland Gazette*)
A Guide to the Pennine Way—C. J. Wright (Constable)

CLEVELAND WAY
Maps
1:50,000 sheets 93, 94, 99, 100, 101

185

Guides
Cleveland Way—Alan Falconer (HMSO)
Cleveland Way—W. Cowley (Dalesman)
Cleveland Way and Missing Link—Malcolm Boyes (Constable)

NORTH DOWNS WAY
Maps
OS 1:50,000 sheets 178, 179, 186, 187, 188, 189
Guides
A Guide to the North Downs Way and Pilgrims Way—C. J. Wright
  (Constable)
Leaflet on *Hollingbourne to Dover Section*—Kent CC, County Hall,
  Maidstone

SOUTH DOWNS WAY
Maps
OS 1:50,000 sheets 197, 198, 199
Guides
Along the South Downs Way—Eastbourne Rambling Club, 28
  Kinfauns Avenue, Eastbourne, East Sussex
South Downs Way—Ernest G. Green (Ramblers' Association)
Walks along the South Downs Way—Lord Teviot (Spurbooks)

SOUTH WEST WAY
Maps
OS 1:50,000 sheets 180, 181, 190, 192, 193, 194, 195, 200, 201,
  202, 203, 204
Guides
Cornwall Coast Path—Edward C. Pyatt (HMSO)
Coastal Path Guide—new edition annually from South West Way
  Association, Beaver Lodge, Rundle Road, Newton Abbot, Devon.
The South-West Peninsula Coast Path, 1 Minehead to St. Ives, 2 St.
  Ives to Plymouth, 3 Plymouth to Poole—Ken Ward and John
  H. N. Mason (Charles Letts)

OFFA'S DYKE PATH
Maps
OS 1:50,000 sheets 116, 117, 126, 137, 148, 161, 162
    (See also strip maps below)
Guides
Offa's Dyke Path—John B. Jones (HMSO)
Offa's Dyke—Frank Noble (Offa's Dyke Association, Knighton,
  Powys LD7 1EW)
Offa's Dyke Path—Arthur Roberts (Ramblers' Association)
Offa's Dyke Path—C. J. Wright (Constable)
Offa's Dyke Strip Maps (1:25,000)—Tony Drake (Offa's Dyke
  Association)

PEMBROKESHIRE COAST PATH
Maps
OS 1:50,000 sheets 145, 157, 158
Guide
Pembrokeshire Coast Path—John Barratt (HMSO)

RIDGEWAY PATH
Maps
OS 1:50,000 sheets 165, 173, 174, 175
Guides
The Ridgeway Path—Séan Jennett (HMSO)
A Practical Guide to Walking the Ridgeway Path—H. D. Westacott
  (Footpath Publications)
The Oldest Road: an exploration of the Ridgeway—J. R. L.
  Anderson (Wildwood House)

DALES WAY
Maps
OS 1:50,000 sheets 96, 98, 99, 104
Guide
The Dales Way—Colin Speakman (Dalesman)

COAST TO COAST WALK
Maps
OS 1:50,000 sheets 89, 90, 91, 92, 93, 94, 98, 99
Guide
A Coast to Coast Walk—A. Wainwright (*Westmorland Gazette*)

VIKING WAY
Maps
OS 1:50,000 sheets 112, 113, 121, 122, 130
Guides
Leaflets describing part of the route available from Lincolnshire CC,
  County Hall, Lincoln

WOLDS WAY
Maps
OS 1:50,000 sheets 100, 101, 106, 107
Guides
Wolds Way—David Rubinstein (Dalesman)
Wolds Way Accommodation and Transport Guide—RA East Yorks
  and Derwent Area (Geoff Eastwood, 60 Front Street, Lockington,
  Driffield, Humberside)

ESSEX WAY
Maps
OS 1:50,000 sheets 167, 168
Guide
Essex Way (CPRE, 79 Springfield Road, Chelmsford, Essex)

WEALDWAY
Maps
OS 1:50,000 sheets 177, 188, 198, 199
Guides
Wealdway—Gravesend to Tonbridge (Meopham Publications Committee, Wrenbury, Wrotham Road, Hook Green, Meopham, Kent)
Wealdway—Tonbridge to Uckfield (Geoffrey King, Fox House, Hadlow Stair, Tonbridge, Kent TN10 4HB)

LONDON COUNTRYWAY
Maps
OS 1:50,000 sheets 165, 166, 167, 175, 177, 186, 187, 188
Guide
The London Countryway—Keith Chesterton (Constable)

COTSWOLD WAY
Maps
OS 1:50,000 sheets 150, 151, 163, 172, 173
Guide
Cotswold Way: a walker's guide—Mark Richards (Thornhill Press)

NORTH BUCKS WAY
Maps
OS 1:50,000 sheets 152, 165
Guide
North Bucks Way—(Ramblers' Association Southern Area, Crawford Mews, York Street, London W1H 1PT)

OXFORDSHIRE WAY
Maps
Set of three maps, scale 1:25,000, from CPRE, Sandford Mount, Charlbury, Oxon

TWO MOORS WAY
Maps
OS 1:50,000 sheets 180, 181, 191, 202
Guide
Two Moors Way—RA Devon Area (J. R. Turner, 'Coppins', The Poplars, Pinhoe, Exeter)

188

Acknowledgements

Photographic illustrations are from the following sources, to whom acknowledgement is gratefully made:
Tom Stephenson, pp10, 15, 36; Geoffrey Berry, pp12, 76, 145, 148–9, 160; *Manchester Evening News*, p35; Peter Nevell, p61; Brian Anderson, p67; British Tourist Authority, p68; Evelyn Durrant, pp70–1; Miss A. Clarke, p74; David Sharp, pp 78–9, 126, 131, 133; *Yorkshire Post*, p89; YHA Services, p94; Helly Hansen, p96; Scout Shops, p99; W. A. J. Finn, pp104–5; Miss Pattinson, pp116–17; Forestry Commission, pp138, 169; Crown Copyright, p143; English Tourist Board, p144; *British Farmer and Stockbreeder*, p170.

Index

192